You Have
3 Minutes!

You Have 3 Minutes!

Foreword by
DONALD TRUMP

LEARN THE SECRET OF THE PITCH FROM TRUMP'S ORIGINAL APPRENTICE

✳ ✳ ✳

RICARDO BELLINO

McGraw-Hill

New York   Chicago   San Francisco   Lisbon   London
Madrid   Mexico City   Milan   New Delhi   San Juan
Seoul   Singapore   Sydney   Toronto

The **McGraw·Hill** Companies

1 2 3 4 5 6 7 8 9 0 DOC/DOC 0 9 8 7 6

ISBN 13: 978-0-07-147255-5
ISBN 10: 0-07-147255-X

This publication is designed to provide accurate and authoritative information in regard to the subject matter covered. It is sold with the understanding that the publisher is not engaged in rendering legal, accounting, or other professional service. If legal advice or other expert assistance is required, the services of a competent professional person should be sought.
> —*From a Declaration of Principles Jointly Adopted by a Committee of the American Bar Association and a Committee of Publishers and Associations*

McGraw-Hill books are available at special discounts to use as premiums and sales promotions, or for use in corporate training programs. For more information, please write to the Director of Special Sales, Professional Publishing, McGraw-Hill, Two Penn Plaza, New York, NY 10121-2298. Or contact your local bookstore.

 This book is printed on recycled, acid-free paper containing a minimum of 50% recycled de-inked paper.

Library of Congress Cataloging-in-Publication Data

Bellino, Ricardo.
    You have three minutes! / by Ricardo Bellino.
        p. cm.
    Includes bibliographical references.
    ISBN 0-07-147255-X (alk. paper)
1. Success in business. 2. Business etiquette. 3. Business communication.
4. Intuition. I. Title.
    HF5386.B3755 2006
    650.1—dc22
                                                    2006016097

CONTENTS

ACKNOWLEDGMENTS

During my lifetime, I have had the opportunity to share experiences with rare characters in the world of business, and others who were not so rare. Among the rare characters, I would underscore the real life Midas's, those who change everything they touch for the better and who have the gift of transforming ideas into successful businesses. This is the case of John Casablancas and Donald Trump, with whom I have had the pleasure of working and learning—and I take advantage of this moment to thank these mentors who truly inspired me in life and in business.

And to the not-so-rare characters, like King Sadim ("Sadim" is Midas written backwards), who are always so busy trying to attack that which they cannot equal, I also offer my thanks for the motivation they gave me to continue writing success stories.

FOREWORD

If anyone knows how much I value time, it's Ricardo Bellino. I gave him a deadline, he met it, and that was that. We became business partners. I mentioned in my book *Think Like a Billionaire* that Ricardo Bellino had exactly three minutes to give me his business presentation. I was extremely busy that day and not particularly in the mood for a presentation, so I thought he might decline, which would free up my day a bit. Not only did he not decline, he gave me such a great presentation within those three minutes that we became partners. It's surprising what people can do with a deadline. What people don't often realize is that when I say "three minutes," I mean three minutes, and for a good reason. I'm not being dramatic or unreasonable. Ricardo also understood that, and his perception and response to that challenge made his a unique story.

This is a story worth reading, and I would urge you to spend more than three minutes reading it. It deserves your attention, and it will hold your attention. After all, that's what Ricardo Bellino achieved in my office. I'm not known for being easy to please, but a step in the right direction is learning to make the most of good advice. Read, learn, and succeed. It's all here.

—Donald J. Trump

You Have
3 Minutes!

INTRODUCTION

"Eighty percent of success is showing up."
—WOODY ALLEN

It was described in the *New York Times* (May 19, 2004). A young Brazilian businessman was received by Donald Trump and greeted with the following sentence from the billionaire: "You have three minutes to sell me your idea." A short while later, the businessman left Trump's office with a closed deal.

I am that young Brazilian businessman to which the *Times* referred. And the idea was to build the Villa Trump—a half-billion dollar business—the largest and most exclusive golf resort in Latin America and the first enterprise in Brazil bearing the Donald Trump brand.

After the news was released by the press, I realized that Trump's three-minute mandate exerted a very powerful effect over people. Everyone wanted to know how it was possible to close a deal of such magnitude in just three minutes. Later on, of course, I met with Trump's assistants and all of the business details were discussed to exhaustion. But the fact remains that those three minutes played a crucial role in securing the deal. If I had not been able to sell the concept of my idea in that brief period of time, Trump would have summarily dismissed me and would never have asked me to discuss the details with his assistants. But what happened, after all, during those three minutes? How can a handful of seconds have such decisive importance?

While trying to answer those questions, I began to reflect on the subject of what is involved in doing business and to conduct some research. My research delivered very surprising results—I would dare say almost revolutionary—if those results are compared to a more traditional and conservative point of view about the meaning of doing business. Negotiation in business involves:

- The power of intuition

- The ability to make decisions at the snap of a finger

- The impact caused by our first impression of someone

- The internal mechanism that leads us to instantly process a vast amount of objective and subjective information—a mechanism—that scientists call the "adaptive unconscious"

These elements have become the object of study by scientists at the most renowned international institutions. Their research reveals that the acclaimed sentence "You have three minutes to sell me your idea" is not only an impact sentence. Quite the contrary, it is the key to every successful negotiation.

Before buying your idea—a project, a new business, the execution of a certain task, or a promotion—your audience must buy your image. And this happens the moment someone sets eyes on another person for the first time. The impact of this first impression is what will make the other intuitively feel whether that person likes you or not, whether you inspire confidence or not, and whether that person wants you nearby or not. In short, it is the initial positive impression that a person registers about you that will open the door for your idea to be sold successfully.

Surprised—as well as excited—after figuring out the essence of the three minutes, I realized it was now time to get this message out to the general public and demonstrate how to use all of these elements to open doors and obtain success in one's professional life in a simple and practical manner.

In this book, I'll also address the characteristics that define the spirit of an entrepreneur (and the stories of successful people who personify this spirit); the traps that must be avoided along the way; and the lessons learned from Donald Trump's television show, *The Apprentice* (a true lesson in entrepreneurship). Finally, a battery of tests will help you evaluate at what stage of the journey you're in currently and what you still need to complete it.

As for my own journey, I would say this book is an important stage in a cycle that began with my two previous books, *POI: The Power of Ideas* (2003) and *Stone Soup: Ten Ingredients for You to Create Your Recipe for Success* (2004), and reflects my search for my own development as a businessman, as an entrepreneur, and as a human being. To share what I have learned during this journey is one way for me to contribute to the development of the entrepreneurial spirit.

Chapter 1

The SCIENCE BEHIND
The *THREE MINUTES*

———— * ✳ * ————

"It is by science that we prove,
but by intuition that we discover."
—HENRI POINCARÉ,
French scientist and author

The moment you pick up this book, many doubts may rush through your mind:

Sell an idea in three minutes?
How?
Is it really possible?

My answer is that not only is it possible, but it is also the only effective way to sell an idea. It is during those initial moments when you first make contact with the person who will invest in your idea, hire you for a job, acquire your services, or take part in your business that the truly essential things are decided. During this short period of time several factors—many of them subjective and subconscious—will join to allow the other person to extract, process, and register his or her first impression about you.

It is my belief that this first impression is so powerful that it will determine the entire course of events that follow: whether there will be support or opposition, receptivity or rejection, openness or indifference, connection or disconnection, and whether you will be dismissed after a few seconds or you will earn an attentive listener for the next few minutes—or hours. Of course, it will take more than three minutes for you to close your deal. You will need to present your arguments, and the investor, client, or employer may ask for some time to think and reflect. However, that is a later stage, and you can only reach that stage successfully if the other party has had a favorable first impression about you during those first three minutes.

Almost all successful people, if not all, have a very sharp intuition that allows them to take utmost advantage of their first impressions. Conrad Hilton, the founder of the Hilton hotel chain, used to say he used his intuition to decide where and when he should buy or build a hotel. Thomas Edison bragged about listening to his "inner voice" in his search for ideas for new inventions. Sílvio Santos, the Brazilian TV show host and one of the richest men in Brazil, who began his career as a street vendor and ended up building an empire, is known to make one-minute intuitive decisions. Salim Mattar, the founder of Localiza, one of the largest car rental companies in Brazil, is not ashamed to say, "At times I simply send shivers down the spines of my peers when I say I won't do something because my intuition advises against it." Even Albert Einstein once commented that a large part of his discoveries were derived from "good hunches." At a Global Leadership Conference lunch meeting, Jack Welch, considered to be the "executive of the century," once said that if there is one thing he truly regrets, it is not having made some of his decisions faster.

The impact of first impressions is so powerful that there is even a company in the United States with that exact name: First Impressions. Founded by two psychologists, Ann DeMarais and Valerie White, the company trains clients in the art of the making the best possible impression, whether for professional, social, or personal reasons. "The first thing you notice or find out about someone weighs a lot more than anything you find out later," say the two psychologists in their book *First Impressions: What You Don't Know About How Others See You* (New York: Bantam, 2004).

The weight of a first positive or negative impression doesn't affect professional relationships only; it also influences romantic relationships. This premise led to the formation of Hurry Date, a company created in New York with the objective of bringing together people in search of romantic partners or new friendships. The thing that distinguishes Hurry Date from so many other agencies of its kind is that everything has to work out in just three minutes. In the events promoted by the company, each participant has exactly three minutes to talk to each of the other participants. After time has run out, a whistle blows, and the people have to stop their conversation and begin to talk with another participant. At the end of each conversation, a secret file card is filled out where the person says whether he liked his partner or not. After that, Hurry Date cross-indexes the information from the file cards and puts together those participants whose evaluations of each other matched. But why three minutes? According to the founders of Hurry Date, that is the amount of time necessary for a person to decide whether there was a spark or an attraction. That way, they claim, their clients avoid that uneasy feeling so common in blind dates—having to spend long hours in conversation with someone with whom they just did not hit it off.

The Adaptive Unconscious and "Snap-of-the-Finger Decisions"

✳ ✸ ✳

What is truly behind all this after all? Could it be that the age-old adage "The first impression is the one that lasts" is really true? Modern science seems to indicate this to be the case. Over the past few years, a large number of neuroscientists and psychologists have dedicated themselves to studying the mechanism that leads us to, among other things, make intuitive decisions in the blink of an eye; to decide, in just a few seconds, whether we like a certain person or not; and to form a mental image, or even an opinion about something or someone, based on our first impressions.

This mechanism has a name: it is called the *adaptive unconscious*. According to Timothy D. Wilson, professor of psychology at the University of Virginia and author of the book *Strangers to Ourselves: Discovering the Adaptive Unconscious*, this mechanism can be defined as a mental process that is inaccessible to consciousness but that influences judgments, feelings, behavior, and decisions. Also, according to Wilson, the adaptive unconscious processes information, establishes objectives, judges people,

8

detects danger, formulates stereotypes, and infers causes. More-over, there is a good reason for all of this to happen without our awareness. "The process is occult for the good of efficiency," explains the professor. We need to process so much information to survive that some of this must be done unconsciously. Even when the mind is occupied with something else, the unconscious mind is working.

One of the experiments conducted by Wilson gives us a clearer idea of how this works in practice. In one of his tests, he asked a group of people to choose one of several posters on exhibit. The choice had to be fast, based only on the instinctive reaction of affinity or repulsion that the images in the posters caused. A second group was told to do the same. However, this group would use a different approach: the members of this group could stand before a poster for long periods of time and think about the reasons that led them to like or dislike each poster. After a few weeks, it was observed that the people in the first group, those who had made instinctive choices, continued liking the posters they had chosen and wanted to keep them, whereas in the second group the exact opposite took place. Most of the people who had more time to analyze and reflect on their preferences ended up changing their minds later, regretting their first choice.

What this and other similar experiments seem to indicate is that while acting beneath our conscious thoughts, the adaptive unconscious is able to instantly gather and process a set of infor-mation, compare it to our likes, desires, inclinations, and most pro-found motivations, and come back with an instinctive answer, such as "I like," "I don't like," "I want," or "I don't want;" "yes" or "no." On the other hand, the conscious mind does not always have the means to gather the same amount of information gathered by the unconscious at the same speed. It tends to favor some aspects to the detriment of others and to include analyses in the process that do not always have our most profound instincts as the point of origin. In other words, it resorts to our "intellectual database" and not necessarily our "emotional database." It is therefore easy to understand why a large percentage of the people with more time to choose a poster ended up regretting the choice they had made.

Another surprising study was carried out by Nalini Ambady, who has a Ph.D. in social psychology and is a professor at Tufts University in Massachusetts. In an experiment reported in the book *Blink: The Power of Thinking Without Thinking* by Malcolm Gladwell, Professor Ambady exhibited images of two seconds' duration to a group of people, without any sound, showing professors that they had never seen before teaching classes. After that, she asked the participants to evaluate the professors based on the feelings the images had generated in them. As amazing as it may seem, the evaluations were essentially the same as those made by students who had had classes with these professors over an entire semester!

According to the Tufts professor, "Three seconds are sufficient for us to form an impression about someone we have just met." Humans developed the skill to decide quickly whether a new acquaintance will "harm us or enrich us." She explains: "In the past, 'snap decisions' meant the difference between life and death." The professor affirms that these instant impressions are generated in the most primitive area of the brain, where feelings are also processed, and that is what leads to the emotional impact caused by a first meeting.

Therefore, we can say that snap decisions are part of a defense mechanism, developed during a time when humans had to decide quickly whether an approaching stranger was friend or enemy—at the risk of losing their own life if they thought too long about it. Nowadays, this mechanism manifests itself in many other aspects: in the distrust we feel with regard to a salesperson who comes knocking at our door or the instant affinity we feel for a new commercial partner; in the feeling that someone is going to be an eternal source of headaches or the gut feeling that an unknown someone is the right person for the job.

"The first impression is an emotional, not a rational, reaction. That's why it is so profound and powerful," says Professor Frank Bernieri, a social psychologist from Oregon State University. He says that all of the aspects of a person's personality are incorporated in his or her behavior, and that a perfect stranger can detect these aspects in a quick and instinctive manner. His thesis is well-supported by his experiments. In one of them, volunteers evaluated the sociability, affability, responsibility, emotional stability, and cultural level of people they had never seen before—and all in an instantaneous and intuitive manner. To do this, Bernieri filmed the participants who would be evaluated in two situations. In the first, a stranger asks the participant to simply give his opinion about a painting. In the second, the participant interacts with another stranger, but this time a person whose behavior is irritating. After that, the volunteers are shown videos of these situations, each running only ten seconds. Once again, the results were surprising. The volunteers were able to evaluate all five aspects of each participant's personality with an amazing degree of precision.

Right about now, you may be asking yourself, "So you mean our intuition never betrays us? Are first impressions never wrong?" The answer to the first question is, "No, intuition never betrays us." *We* are the ones who betray *it*. Intuition does not always tell us what we want to hear. It may tell us that the person we are in love with is not the right person for us, that the business that looks like an irresistible opportunity is nothing more than a trap, or that the object we want so much to buy is nothing more than a white elephant. Then, rather than listen to our intuition, we manipulate it unconsciously, and we ignore all of the warning signs that something is just not right for the simple reason that we *want* it to be right. It is the same old game of fooling yourself, and the first step in learning how to use one's intuition as a successful person is to be able to identify these situations and deal with them. Other factors also count. People with low self-esteem and high levels of insecurity, melancholy, or depression tend to trust their intuition less.

Consequently, the answer to the second question is: Yes, first impressions can often be wrong. As Professor Bernieri warns, "A person's personality is faithfully coded in the first thirty seconds of his behavior, which does not mean that people pick up on it accurately all the time."[1]

Learning to Impress Positively

* ※ *

From a professional perspective, I would say that there are two important lessons we can extract from all this. The first one is: Intuition is an extremely important tool. The sharper it is, the

---

[1] See http://money.cnn.com/2000/09/01/people/q_firstimpression.

more successful you will be. To increasingly sharpen your intuition is equivalent to trusting yourself more, to listening to your inner voice, which connects you to your deepest instincts. How to do this is something you will find out in this book.

The second lesson is: First impressions may be wrong, but they still leave their mark. Therefore, don't waste your time trying to prove to other people that they were wrong about you. Instead, be more concerned about making a good impression from the very beginning.

Few things are more difficult and draining than trying to convince people that their first impression was wrong, and with good reasons. The many studies mentioned above indicate that first impressions are much more powerful than we could ever imagine because they are connected to a defense and protection mechanism that human beings have developed in order to survive as a species.

Thus, instead of fighting against this, a person geared toward success should be concerned about making a good impression right off the bat—especially when you consider that the first impression a person will have about you may just be your only chance. How could you convince a human resources interviewer who for some reason had an unfavorable impression about you during a job interview that he or she is wrong and that you are the right person for the job? How could you convince an investor who did not hit it off with you that your project is excellent? How could I ever try to convince Donald Trump that his instincts were mistaken if no empathy had arisen between us when he told me, "You have three minutes to sell me your idea?"

The main problem involved in taking on these types of impossible—or nearly impossible—missions is that many times we do not even realize we caused an unfavorable impression, much less the reasons for why it happened. We think, "But my project was perfect!" or "I had all the necessary qualifications for that job," or even "I have no doubt in my mind I was ready for that promotion," without realizing that the problem is much more complex. Even before our projects, ideas, merits, and qualifications are evaluated, our personality has already been judged. As we have seen, this evaluation is made by the adaptive unconscious, and as such, it is quick, instinctive, and happens at the exact moment two people meet for the first time. Moreover, if, for some reason, we fail in this evaluation, it is very unlikely we will ever be able to pass on to the second stage, which is when our projects, ideas, merits, and qualification are actually evaluated.

The good news is that you can and should control the first impression you create. Proof of this is in the existence of companies such as Hurry Date and First Impressions and, of course, the experiences of businessmen such as myself. After all, I was able to sell my idea to Donald Trump in the three minutes he allotted me.

You might protest, "But I have no charisma, I just wasn't born with a magnetic personality." It is true that some people seem to have the "gift" of creating a favorable impression in a natural manner without the least effort. However, that is because they developed the skill to deal with a series of factors that help to project their favorable image. These factors range from knowing themselves to sharpening their intuition, and they include verbal and nonverbal communication, the capacity to create empathy, to transmit confidence, to know how to listen, and to demonstrate genuine interest in the other person, and so on. And if those people can do it, you can too. That is what I will share with you in this book.

Intuition versus Strategy: Keep Both

* ✳ *

After everything that I've said about intuition, instinct, adaptive unconscious, snap decisions, and first impressions, it is important to underscore that none of these elements is a substitute for strategy and planning. In reality, they complement one another. Knowing how to balance all of these elements is the great secret to selling an idea in three minutes.

If making a favorable first impression is the key that opens the door, it is fundamental to think about what to do before and after. What do I do to get to that door? And what do I do after crossing the threshold?

Reaching the door means knowing how to take advantage of, and how to create, opportunities. And that involves a combination of intuition and strategy. Knowing what to do after crossing the threshold means presenting content that is worthy of the favorable impression you created or, in other words, doing a good job and proving yourself worthy of the confidence intuitively vested in you. And here the only way intuition will not be of help is if it is not accompanied with discipline and planning. Whereas a negative impression is difficult to be changed, a positive impression is not all that hard to be reversed. In most cases, all the other person needs to do is realize you are not worthy of the confidence that has been deposited, you are not fulfilling what was promised, or you are not behaving in a manner that corresponds to the positive image projected in the beginning.

The effects of this are even worse than creating an unfavorable first impression. In the case of an unfavorable impression, what could occur is that the person in question could miss out on the opportunity to close a deal, to sell an idea, to get a job, or to begin a romantic relationship. But that doesn't prevent the person from reflecting on the causes of the problem and learning to transmit a positive image in other circumstances or to other people—or even to the same people should the opportunity arise. However, when someone creates a favorable image and then does not prove worthy of it, he or she ends up establishing a feeling of deception or unease. The other person begins to feel betrayed or fooled, and the person who caused this ends up getting the reputation of being unreliable or just plain untrustworthy. This situation is much more difficult to revert, because even if people try to change their image under different circumstances, with different people, their reputation will have preceded them. Other people will have formed a negative impression about them even before they have ever had the chance to meet.

Therefore, creating and maintaining a good reputation is the first step toward making a good first impression, and to accomplish that, intuition alone will not be enough. Intuition can tell you who you can trust; it can give you the "gut feeling" that a business is good or not, that it is time to take a risk or to act with caution, that something has a chance at working or failing, and so on. In short, it can help you open the first door, the entrance gate. However, to build relationships, to solidify ideas, to consolidate professional success, and make businesses work, intuition operates hand in hand with sensitivity, planning, strategic thinking, perseverance, and discipline.

The night I heard my friend describe the characteristics of a piece of land that was for sale just outside São Paulo, my intuition led me to make a snap decision: I was going to sell Donald Trump on the idea of creating the largest golf condo in Latin America right there on the spot. However, it was from that initial intuition that I developed a series of studies and surveys with the purpose of being able to present a detailed and valuable project. In other words, I didn't just walk up to the American billionaire and say, "Hey, how about building a golf complex in Brazil?" That would be confusing intuition with impulsiveness, which is something totally different. To act driven by intuition has nothing to do with being driven by impulse. Intuition is the inner voice, and it is connected to the adaptive unconscious. That means it doesn't just jump up out of nowhere. It originates in the processes that take place in the shadows of consciousness. On the other hand, an impulse can come from anywhere, even from a whim or some passing interest.

After conceiving the idea and studying its feasibility, I devised a strategic plan to reach Donald Trump. A fundamental factor in this was the letter John Casablancas, the founder of the world-famous Elite Model Agency, wrote introducing me to Trump. Casablancas wrote this letter thanks to the relationship we had developed as partners in implementing the Brazilian branch of Elite Models 18 years earlier. That means that when Trump conceded me those famous three minutes, I had already been preceded by a good reputation. Naturally, that was a positive factor. However, a good reputation alone would have been worthless if Trump had not had a favorable first impression of me. At the very most, he might have thought, "I don't get what it is Casablancas ever saw in this guy."

At the end of the three minutes, Trump asked George Ross, executive vice president and senior counsel for The Trump Organization, and his advisers to discuss the project with me in the other room, telling them "Do not leave there until a deal has been reached." I had made a favorable first impression and the door was now open. But that also would have been worthless if I hadn't presented a consistent, feasible, and promising project to Ross and the megabusinessman's advisers. If I hadn't prepared myself for that moment and had simply relied on my intuition to tell me what to do to get on Ross's good side, I probably would have left that room in less than three minutes, without reaching any deal at all.

When Luck Is a Matter of Talent

* * *

In all of the other phases of consolidating the Villa Trump, which would be the American billionaire's first enterprise outside of the United States, I used the same combination of intuition and strategic planning. That was how I endeavored to approach the investors, to choose the collaborators, and to gather all the right people to make the project possible. When things work out, many times we think of that famous line, "The universe conspires in your favor." Everything just seems to fall into place; coincidences seem to make the path easier, and luck seems to be on our side. Who hasn't had that feeling?

But, if we really think about it, the so-called conspiracy of the universe is nothing mystical or supernatural; nothing benefits us in some random manner without our having done anything for it to happen. We did do something, and probably a lot. We intuited, planned, persisted, worked, kept our convictions concerning our purposes, and despite all the obstacles, we never let our enthusiasm wane. And then, all of the efforts begin to pay off. The right people appeared, not out of luck, but because we attracted them with our enthusiasm. Opportunities arise not by chance, but because we have laid the groundwork for them to arise. This concept can be summarized as follows: Many people believe that to have talent is a matter of luck; however, very few think that luck itself may very well be a matter of talent.

Therefore, to sell an idea within a three-minute time frame is not a matter of luck. It is a matter of knowing how to listen to intuition, knowing how to prepare, knowing how to create a good impression, and knowing how to live up to the expectations. And, as you will see in this book, this can all be learned and improved.

Chapter 2

BUSINESS And
INTUITION

* ✳ *

*"When I make a decision of little importance,
I always find it advantageous to ponder
all the pros and cons. However, when it comes
to vital issues, such as choosing a female companion
or a profession, the decision has to come from
the unconscious, from somewhere inside of us.
In the important decisions of our personal lives,
I believe we must be governed by the
deepest inner needs of our nature."*
—SIGMUND FREUD

Intuition is not only one of the indispensable factors in *selling* an idea in three minutes, it is also fundamental in *buying* a good idea in three minutes. If you are the person doing the selling, your success depends on a set of elements that are discussed throughout this book, such as the image you project, the discourse you present, the way your idea is structured, the knowledge you have about the potential buyer, and several other elements. However, intuition is the mortar that joins all these elements, and that is why many sales books, courses, and training programs do not achieve their objectives. You may know all of the commandments of a good salesman by heart and you may strive to apply them word for word, but without a sharpened and intuitive sensitivity about how you present the more technical elements of the idea, the whole thing will have a hard time getting off the ground.

The reason is easy to understand. You are not merely pouring data into a computer. You are dealing with human beings and all of their subtleties and idiosyncrasies, their moods and beliefs, their preferences and opinions, their fears and desires, their backgrounds, and their views of the world. Communication, speech, and interpersonal relationship courses may assist you, but the bottom line is that they can only indicate paths and supply a few parameters. Because intuition is connected to the adaptive consciousness, which as we saw in the previous chapter is capable of instantly processing countless pieces of objective and subjective information, it is what makes the difference when it comes time to deal with all of the complexities of a human being. That is what is in play during those few seconds you have to make a good first impression. And, if you are not in tune with your own intuition, all of the manuals and workshops in the world will not help you.

With regard to the investor, employer, or buyer who is on the other side of the table, factors such as experience, knowledge, vision, and emotional equilibrium are key when it comes time to close a deal, choose a partner, hire an employee, assume a risk, take advantage of opportunities, or make a decision. However, I once again insist that without intuition it is highly unlikely that satisfactory results would be achieved. In general, people tend to see successful men and women as "special" people, as the "chosen" or "lucky" ones. But, in reality, the great differential is the fact that they have sharpened their intuition and they are always, or frequently, in tune with it.

The economist, Herbert Simon, winner of the Nobel Prize for Economics in 1978, researched the role of intuition in the decisions made in the business world. Based on his studies, he concluded that people who are experts in their area make decisions that result from a combination of intuition and logical thinking. Another conclusion from his studies is that intuition can be more accurately described as the product of a subconscious mental activity.

Among the many examples I could cite to illustrate Simon's conclusions is the case of megainvestor George Soros. Soros's son Robert once said in a *Wall Street Journal* interview, "My father will sit down and give you theories to explain why he does this or that. But I remember seeing it as a kid and thinking . . . at least half of this is bullsh--. I mean, the reason he changes his position on the market or whatever is because his back starts killing him. It has nothing to do with reason." In other words, for Soros, his intuition communicates with him through the pain in his back. It isn't only about his knowledge of the market, his contacts, and his information network that guide him, but there is also—and most important of all—the signals his intuition sends him. This theme became an object of interest to a Brazilian economist living in New York, Flávia Cymbalista. She also has a doctorate degree in cognitive psychology from the University of Berkeley, and she produced a study with the very curious title *How George Soros Knows What He Knows* that underscores Soros's reliance on his intuition when making business decisions.

Soros is far from an isolated case. While still a student, Frederick Smith showed one of his college professors a project about a new rapid delivery service. The professor was not the least bit enthused with the project and gave the student a C. Despite the professor's discouraging reaction, Smith—who intuitively believed in his idea—decided to go ahead with it. That is how he founded Federal Express, transforming the idea into a $29 billion business.

Intuition also played an important role in the life of Howard Schultz, who in the beginning of the 1980s worked as marketing director for Starbucks, a Seattle-based company that supplied coffee to bars and restaurants. On a trip to Milan, Schultz was calmly sitting in a café when he was suddenly overcome by a very powerful sense of intuition. He simply "knew" that the café style of coffeehouse could become an unprecedented success. That intuitive moment was so strong that Schultz remembers that he actually trembled with emotion. Schultz ended up buying Starbucks, transforming it into an international network of coffeehouses. Today, each week, approximately 33 million people go drink their coffee at one of the many Starbucks in just about every corner of the planet.

Fletcher L. Byrom, former CEO for Koppers Company, a multinational that operates in the chemical sector, once said, "I have found that some of the most horrible mistakes we have made came after I ignored my intuition, under the pressure of what looked, at the time, like unshakable evidence." And Bill Gates himself has admitted, "Often you have to rely on intuition."[2]

---

[2] See http://www.businesspotential.com/intuition.pdf for Byrom's quote. For Gates's quote, see http://quotesandsayings.com/billgates.htm.

If that is how it is, then why is intuition still viewed with a certain amount of skepticism? It just so happens, that although it is as old as mankind, intuition has only recently been studied in a scientific way. According to Timothy Wilson, a researcher from the University of Virginia known for his work on the adaptive unconscious, for many years scientists have been reluctant to study the unconscious because it was very difficult to do so with reliable scientific methods. With the emergence of new methods, such as studies on perception and learning and attention processes, the study of the unconscious began to attract the interest of several top scientists, including Ph.D.'s from Harvard, the Massachusetts Institute of Technology, Tufts University, and several other internationally renowned institutions.

The results of these studies have helped shed new light on intuition. What was seen before as something vague and obscure, bearing a certain mystical aura, is now being studied under the light of modern science. Intuition is considered to be part of an unconscious mental process that can be a valuable tool when it is necessary to make quick decisions under pressure, distinguish the best option among a multitude of choices, detect opportunities, and find innovative and creative solutions. This change is reflected in a recent study by the International Institute for Management Development (IMD), an entity headquartered in Switzerland. Eighty percent of the executives from nine countries who were interviewed said that intuition had become an important element in formulating corporate strategy and planning. And 53 percent declared that they rely on intuition and logical reasoning equally in their day-to-day work.

Intuition Doesn't Stop Talking to Us— We Stop Listening

* ✳ *

Even with all the studies and evidence that point to the importance of intuition in our everyday lives, there is still some prejudice surrounding the subject. Some believe that being rational or intuitive is necessarily opposite and exclusive. They believe that the adjective *rational* suggests some sort of intellectual superiority, while the term *intuitive* implies a lack of formal knowledge or academic instruction. But history shows that this is not the case. There are countless examples of ingenious scientists, gifted with deep knowledge and indisputable intellectual capacity, who used intuition to find the key to a problem or to make discoveries that influenced all of humanity.

In ancient Syracuse, Archimedes, considered to be one of the greatest mathematicians of all times, had an insight while visiting a bathhouse. He noticed that the volume of water that shifted every time he entered the bath was equivalent to the volume of his immersed body. Archimedes thus discovered a principle that would allow him to measure the volume of an object based on the amount of water it displaced. The story goes that Archimedes was in such ecstasy over his discovery that he began to run about naked in the streets, shouting the now famous "Eureka!" That's why until today someone says "Eureka" when the solution to a problem is found in an intuitive, unexpected, and sudden way.

It is interesting to observe that Archimedes had been working on the issue of measuring volumes for quite some time. But it was during a moment of distraction, when he was relaxing in the bath that the solution occurred to him in the form of intuition. This and several other similar cases suggest to us that if it is important to use logical reasoning, it is also important to know how to stop and listen to one's intuition. It is difficult, if not impossible, to listen to it when our mind is operating at full steam, grinding away incessantly on some problem. To paraphrase a quote attributed to Albert Einstein, "No problem is solved in the same state as it was created."

In my professional career, I witnessed this fact countless times. In the mid-1990s I was about to open a branch of the Criativa advertising agency, originally founded by Roberto Figueiredo, in Espírito Santo, in São Paulo. When I met with Figueiredo to discuss the details of my participation in the enterprise, I realized Criativa wasn't ready to compete in the largest advertising market in the country. To do this, the company would have to become better known; we first needed to create a success story. That is when I proposed we license the name and image of John Casablancas, my friend and former partner. Figueiredo liked the idea, and with a burst of creative energy, we set out on our first challenge: to launch and position John Casablancas in a way that would then enhance our own public image. After much research we concluded that Casablancas was an extraordinary international cultural figure. We presented the idea to Caio Túlio Costa, then director of *Folha Magazine*, and four weeks later launched the first column signed by John Casablancas. The idea gained momentum and sparked the creation of the Elite Press news agency, which began to supply behind-the-scenes details about the world of fashion for magazines and newspapers in several countries.

The initial impact of these initiatives was very encouraging, suggesting that our venture had every reason to work. Famous last words. All of a sudden, Casablancas decided to move to Rio de Janeiro with his entire family. Feeling that he and his name were overexposed in Brazil, he then resolved to pull out of the project. That news was devastating to Figueiredo and me. There was nothing left for us to do except cancel the whole thing. I can still remember that Friday when I met with Figueiredo in our São Paulo office to define the details for shutting down our activities. Figueiredo left before me, and I stayed behind alone, organizing my documents and files.

Up until that moment, I had sought desperately for a solution to save our company. However, no matter how much I thought about it, not a single idea emerged. So I stopped thinking about the whole thing and went about packing my things. That's when I picked up a clipping about a campaign for the prevention of breast cancer from Elite Press that was sitting on top of a pile of papers. The campaign had just been launched in New York by America's most prominent stylists. All of Elite's top models at the time—Cindy Crawford, Claudia Schiffer, and Naomi Campbell, among others—were the poster girls for the campaign and sold T-shirts designed by Ralph Lauren for the campaign. My mind reeled: why not bring this campaign to Brazil? Why not make it the product launch case for Criativa? It was my turn to shout "Eureka!" The moment I stopped thinking exhaustively about what to do, the solution appeared. And what a solution! I had not only found the ideal case for launching the São Paulo branch of the Criativa agency, but I had also come across the answer to a personal yearning that had been eating away at me for some time: the desire to direct my creativity and my capacity as an entrepreneur to some sort of enterprise that contributed to society, where the return would not be measured by numbers alone, but by its contribution to the improvement of the society in which we live.

Without wasting any time, I called Casablancas' secretary in New York and asked her to get me more information about the campaign and its organizers. In thirty minutes, I received a fax with a complete press kit; I sent a copy to Figueiredo, who was in Rio de Janeiro. He called me soon after to say he had read the material and made the pronouncement, "Bellino has just found a way out for our business and an opportunity to turn things around completely." And that is exactly what happened.

After that initial moment of intuition that showed me which way to go, it was time to start the strategic planning and dig into the details. Knowing when to recognize this moment is a fundamental factor for you to be successful in selling your idea in three minutes. Figueiredo bought my idea immediately. But everything would have been hugely disappointing for both of us if my survival instinct—my intuition—hadn't kicked in. If it is necessary to stop for a moment to listen to your intuition, it is also necessary to get to work as soon as you have heard it. After all, as Pablo Picasso reportedly said, "I have no idea when inspiration is going to come. All I can be sure of is that it will find me hard at work."

I immediately contacted the organizers of the American campaign, the CFDA (Council of Fashion Designers of America), to try to get a license to use the logo and a legitimate association between the initiatives in the two countries. We were able to set an appointment with the top executives at CFDA through the Elite office in New York, and John Casablancas accompanied us. Despite Casablancas' support, the campaign coordinators, which included big names such as Ralph Lauren, Donna Karan, Calvin Klein, and Oscar de la Renta, among others, were concerned about launching an initiative to be handled by strangers in a distant country that was out of their control. The licensing contract took almost three months to be signed, and the task of persuading them to sign it is an example of how strategic intelligence, which I will discuss in later chapters, can be used in your favor.

Upon returning to Brazil, our mission was to find a T-shirt manufacturer with national distribution and a renowned institution with prestige in breast cancer research. I sought support from several sectors, including my friend Costanza Pascolatto, who has great prestige in the national and international fashion press. Coincidentally, Costanza herself was a breast cancer survivor. She was very moved by the idea and contributed to the campaign, offering her relationship network. And this is where another theme that will be discussed in this book comes in: the use of social intelligence to create contacts.

After that, I went about the task of finding a partner in the textile sector that would provide the necessary logistics to produce, distribute, and market the famous T-shirt with the blue target. My first meeting was with Fábio Hering, the president of the clothing manufacturer Hering. He tried to discourage me at first, claiming that such an initiative would not be successful in Brazil because we didn't have the same culture as the Americans in these kinds of ventures. But my intuition kept telling me the project would work, so I did not give up. Then I had to sell him on the idea of creating a partnership: I would buy the T-shirts and would be responsible for reselling them. After taking out the production and campaign administration costs, the amount destined for donation would be given to a philanthropic institution linked to the breast cancer issue. This would all be duly accomplished by an independent auditing company. Now we needed an institution that could complement the partnership. And once again, my intuition came into play.

I received a direct-mail solicitation at home one day asking for donations to the IBCC (Brazilian Institute of Cancer Control), which I did not even know existed at the time, but I felt it could very well be the partner we were seeking. I immediately called the funding director, and found out (to my great surprise) that the IBCC specialized in treating breast cancer, and that the founder of the Institute, Doctor Sampaio Góes, was the doctor who had treated Constanza Pascolatto. I realized that a true "conspiracy" had been formed in favor of the project. And so, with the enthusiasm of the national fashion professionals, the partnership with Hering, and the license that the CFDA granted the IBCC, we created an incredible synergy.

We received tremendous support from the media, who were enthusiastic about our initiative and granted us free space on television, radio, newspapers, magazines, billboards, and everywhere else imaginable. To have an idea of the initiative's potential impact, I obtained 150 pages of free advertising in the most important magazines in the country, in addition to the huge volume of editorial space across mediums. Several personalities loaned their images, further strengthening the campaign. The very first T-shirt was bought by then–First Lady Ruth Cardoso, in a ceremony held at the Itamarati Palace, in Brasília. Mrs. Cardoso asked the entire country to engage in the campaign.

All of this transformed the breast cancer campaign in Brazil into a worldwide phenomenon that was much stronger than the American campaign. The Brazilian initiative, the first outside of the United States, served as a model for franchising the project overseas. To date, the Fashion Targets Breast Cancer campaign has already collected more than 25 million dollars for research and treatment of the disease, and it continues to be successful after ten years, which makes me very proud, even after ending my involvement in the project.

This example demonstrates how intuition is unbeatable when associated with strategic reasoning. The moment of "Eureka!"—the insight I had upon catching sight of the press kit with the American campaign information—was like the spark that lights the flame, so long as the fire has been properly prepared and the spark finds a source to transform itself into a blaze. If the spark had fallen on empty space, it would have extinguished as fast as it had been lit.

Chapter 3

OPTIMIZING
Your
INTUITIVE POWER

* ✳ *

*"I am a great believer in luck,
and I find the harder I work,
the more I have of it."*
—STEPHEN LEACOCK,
Canadian humorist and educator

As we have seen thus far, intuition is one of the key elements in selling an idea in three minutes, as well as many other things. Intuition, or "feeling," is the differential that distinguishes an average businessman from a brilliant one; someone who accumulates an occasional success from a true winner. In this case, we should ask: If we are all naturally intuitive, why do some people seem to be more intuitive than others? Why do certain people demonstrate skill in using intuition in their professional and personal lives, whereas others demonstrate the exact opposite?

The truth of the matter is that just like any instrument, intuition must be finely tuned. Every time we hear a musician play a perfectly tuned instrument it is because before he steps on stage he made the effort to carefully tune his instrument.

Well then, how do we tune intuition?

In the beginning of this book, I said that intuition does not betray us. We are the ones who betray it. Therefore, the first step is to understand how this happens. A good start is to analyze a new version of the experiment I mentioned in the first chapter in which the researcher, Nalini Ambady, from Tufts University, showed two-second videos of professors in the classroom and asked people who had never seen those professors before to evaluate their performances. The evaluations matched those made by the students who had already taken classes with the professors. In a later experiment, Nalini repeated the procedure, with one difference: before making the evaluation, one group watched a comedy scene, while another watched a drama scene. The experiment revealed that the group induced into a more relaxed state after watching the comedy scene was able to evaluate the professors with greater precision than the group induced into a more melancholic state after watching the drama scene. Nalini believes that the people in both groups probably reached the same initial conclusions concerning the professors' evaluations. However, the members of the more melancholic group began to doubt themselves and their instincts and ended up abandoning their first intuitive impressions. This made their evaluations less precise, and in some cases incorrect, when compared to the feedback from the students who really knew the professors.

From that it is possible to infer an important connection between self-esteem and intuition. The lower your self-esteem, the greater the tendency to doubt yourself and, consequently, your intuition. However, the inverse of that attitude can also lead to negative effects. If you hold yourself in such high esteem, to the point where you consider yourself to always be "perfect" and "infallible," this distorted self-image can also distort the way you handle your intuition. Rather than listen to it, you try to manipulate it every time it goes against your desires or intentions. That is not following your intuition; it is following your whims and wants.

Therefore, to fine tune your intuition you must maintain a balanced position, not letting yourself be undermined by low self-esteem, nor be blinded by an arrogant and fanciful image of yourself. Of course it isn't easy to achieve this equilibrium, and I would be lying if I said there is some magic formula. Self-esteem, its absence and its excess, is linked to each individual's life story, and to play around with it means delving into a self-understanding process, which involves our conscious as well as our unconscious motivations.

In his book, *Strangers to Ourselves: Discovering the Adaptive Unconscious*, Timothy Wilson observes that when we try to better understand our unconscious processes, we open the possibility to influence them consciously. In other words, it is possible to direct at least part of this powerful force to, for example, achieve our objectives and goals. Wilson provides insight on how to achieve this: rather than just sitting and thinking about it, it is much more effective to observe your real actions and see to what degree they correspond to your self-image. "For example, people can fool themselves into believing that they are more altruistic than they really are, until they realize that they rarely give money to charity or engage in any volunteer work," he says.

Then he adds, "When they more carefully observe what they do (or don't do), they can revise their theories about their own personalities."

Some unconscious trends and tendencies can be seen as habits that are learned through practice. Therefore, the more we exercise our intuition, the more intuitive we become. And, of course, the more we transform actions and behavior into habits that favor our personal and professional success, the more these habits are incorporated by the unconscious, optimizing our chances for success.

The Characteristics of an Intuitive Person: Do You Have Them?

* ✳ *

The Swiss psychiatrist Carl Jung defined an intuitive person as someone who:

- Observes everything in a holistic manner

- Trusts his or her gut feelings

- Is conscious of the future

- Is imaginative

- Is visionary

If we apply these characteristics to the business world, we will find the detailed profile of successful people in their professions. To *observe everything in a holistic manner* refers to seeing the world with an open mind, noticing how different aspects relate to each other to form a whole. To reach this point, it is crucial to keep all five senses sharpened, for they are the filters through which we receive all external information. If these filters are not working properly, we run the risk of receiving limited, distorted, or erroneous information. In my book, *Stone Soup: Ten Ingredients for You to Create Your Recipe for Success*, I say the following: "We live in a world in which time is measured by a clock, in which rushing and agitation are part of our everyday lives, in which business, work, and commitments absorb us full-time. In this exhaustive routine, the five senses keep getting duller and duller, and what's worse, we barely notice. How many times do we look without seeing, touch without feeling, eat without tasting, hear without listening, and don't even remember we have something called smell?" The five senses are our doors and windows to the world, and there is no way we can look at everything in a holistic manner if the windows are dirty and the doors are locked. Once again citing *Stone Soup*: "The more the five senses are used correctly, the more in tune they become. And the more in tune they become, the sharper your intuition will be. Furthermore, what many people call a 'sixth sense' is, in reality, a sharpened intuition fed by the information that arrives through the five fully developed and opened senses."

The second and third characteristics, trusting gut feelings and being conscious of the future, relate to each other in an interesting manner: one proposes the scope and limits of the other. To say that intuitive people *trust their gut feelings* is the same as saying they have enough self-esteem to believe in themselves and in their inner voice. But how can we be sure this self-esteem will not turn into the arrogance of someone deprived of any self-criticism? The answer is in the next characteristic of an intuitive person, which is being *conscious of the future*. This is not a matter of simply foreseeing the future, but of being aware that it is shaped by the consequence of your actions. In other words, an intuitive person's self-esteem is guided by equilibrium and by the notion of responsibility.

The next characteristics also complement each other. The intuitive person is *imaginative,* because after listening to his or her inner voice, the person gains access to the source of his or her own creativity. However, this capacity to imagine would flow into the realm of fantasies if the intuitive person were not also a *visionary;* that is, someone who can channel and direct his or her imagination.

When I was a student of economics at Cândido Mendes College, in Rio de Janeiro, I was skimming through the pages of the French publication, *Photo Magazine*, one day, and I came across an article about Elite Models, which at the time was the largest modeling agency in the world. The article mentioned "The Look of the Year" contest and highlighted its creator, John Casablancas. Although I was not fluent in French, it wasn't necessary to understand every word to realize that I was faced with a unique opportunity: I intuitively realized I should bring Elite to Brazil. From that moment on, without knowing it, I had already begun to make use of all five characteristics of an intuitive person. Without any doubt, I was able to transform a seemingly absurd idea into a very successful enterprise.

Everyone at college who learned of my intentions thought I had gone nuts. There was no lack of arguments to dissuade me. I heard things like, "But you don't have any money, any contacts, any experience; you're not old enough; you don't speak English; you haven't finished college; you'll never be taken seriously," and so on. It just so happens that I fully believed in my "gut feeling" and that I could find the means to make the idea work. Now, when I think back about everything, I see that all those who tried to discourage me ended up doing me a favor. The opposition I faced helped me realize that there are moments in life when the only thing you can count on is the confidence you have in yourself and in your intuition. And many times that is all that matters.

It was in the wee hours that I began to write a letter to John Casablancas explaining that I saw a wonderful market opportunity. The next day, I asked a friend to translate the letter into English for me. I sent it by telex, but I never received an answer. I sent another telex to confirm whether he had received the first one and I received a message from Casablancas' assistant informing me that he had received my letter and that he would be in touch as soon as he returned from a business trip.

I could never explain the emotion I felt when I received that simple answer, a mixture of excitement and happiness. I realized that written communication would not be enough to express my intentions. That's when I decided to go to New York and present my ideas personally. There is no one better than you to sell your own ideas. Even before I knew how I would arrange my trip, I sent another telex proposing a meeting. To my great surprise, I received a quick reply confirming a meeting with Fernando Casablancas, John's brother, and the person responsible at the time for the operation of the Elite franchises. My expectations were huge, but I didn't have time to sit around wondering what would happen, whether it would work or not. I had to think quickly to find a way to finance my trip to the United States. You see, I had made an appointment with Elite without even having the money to make the trip. It was a way to pressure myself, to make the idea tangible, to think and act at the same time, without hesitating.

If I thought too much about it, I may have ended up acting like the people in the experiment I mentioned in the first chapter, reflecting too long and ending up with regrets. I could have come to the conclusion that according to "logic" the idea would be impossible and would have never set the appointment with Casablancas. But fortunately, I did not fall into that trap. That same day, while reading an article in *Veja* magazine, I found out that DHL, a multinational delivery company, was offering free plane tickets to college students interested in traveling to the United States for a week or two who would work as couriers for the company. I didn't hesitate. I grabbed the phone and called Michael Manion, then president of DHL, who I had met once before when I presented a former project. I told Manion my plans and he immediately confirmed my registration to travel as a courier. With my travel date set, it was time to solve another problem. I didn't have the money to finance the extra expenses for hotels, food, or transportation. The solution was to borrow some money from my father and seek lodging in the most economical place possible, a students' hostel.

Up until now, my conviction that the idea was going to work came from the faith I had in my "gut feeling." But if that was all I had to show Casablancas, I would run the risk of being seen as a foolish and presumptuous young man. And that is how my conscious of the future characteristic manifested itself. To be conscious of the future is much different from dreaming about the future. It means knowing that the future is not the consequence of my dreams, but of my actions. Therefore, I had to transform my initial intuition into a concrete project. Thus, I obtained a purchase option for an abandoned building in São Conrado, in Rio de Janeiro, where the Pote Restaurant once operated; and I was able to have an architect friend of mine, at no cost, prepare a complete proposal for setting up the Elite agency, the John Casablancas modeling schools, a fitness academy, a photo studio, and the Elite fashion café bar and restaurant.

As soon as I arrived in New York, I met a Brazilian who was fluent in English and he agreed to accompany me to the meeting. My first meeting with Fernando Casablancas was very positive. I presented all my plans, blueprints, and videos that showed examples of the beauty of Brazilian women. He explained the details of Elite's operations, and he spoke about the contests and about his franchise network. After that, Fernando was going to evaluate the material, show my plans to John, and give me an answer. One week after returning to Brazil, I received a letter from Fernando to tell me he had made a preliminary analysis of my plans and that he would like to continue our discussions. Without hesitating, I made other trips as a courier to New York in order to meet with him before I ever had the opportunity to meet John Casablancas personally.

However, what Fernando really wanted was to sell me a modeling school franchise, whereas I wanted the option to bring the "Look of the Year" contest to Brazil, and later, the Elite modeling agency. So, he called John in to break our stalemate. When I finally found myself face-to-face with the man who had launched the most celebrated models of the time, and who lived and worked with all those women who were on magazine covers the world over, my anxiety increased even more. Nevertheless, I was able to keep focused. Instead of being intimidated, I treated him as an equal. I summarized my idea, but he, too, tried to sell me a franchise. That's when I told him, "I don't have a penny to my name. I travel to New York as a courier and I stay at the YMCA, therefore, I am in no condition to buy any kind of franchise." He laughed and asked me, "How do you intend to do business with the largest modeling agency in the world without any money?" I answered that I believed tremendously in my idea of taking Elite to Brazil and making it a huge success, and I added that I could find the necessary resources to sponsor the national phase of the contest, and later, to open the Elite Brazil agency. At that same meeting he asked me what I would need to continue moving forward. At the end of our meeting, I asked him for an authorization letter to carry out a feasibility study with support material: catalogs, promotional videos, etc. He promised to get me the material the very next day.

Three months later, I was already thinking he had given up on the idea, when I finally received a package with a letter, a video, and some promotional folders. The next step was to watch the Elite video. Since I didn't have a videocassette player at home, I put the tape in my bag and took it with me to the Fenit, a fashion fair held annually in São Paulo. At the fair, I found a videocassette player at one of the exhibitor's stands and I was able to watch the video about the Elite contest. I stayed there, completely on cloud nine, watching those beautiful images of model candidates and imagining my dream becoming reality. From the very beginning, I had proved to be *imaginative* enough to overcome all the difficulties and to convince Casablancas to give me that option letter. But the time had come for me to prove I was also a *visionary* and that I had sufficient vision to seek opportunities and to make that piece of paper become a real live business.

The opportunity arose just as soon as I left the stand and was approached by a woman who asked me, "Wow, are you from Elite?" She asked me the question because I was wearing an Elite shirt that I myself had made, and that apparently insignificant initiative created an opportunity. The woman would never have approached me if she hadn't identified me as being with Elite. Her name was Vivi Haydu, and she invited me to visit her husband's stand. There, they revealed to me their frustrated attempts at bringing the John Casablancas modeling schools franchise to Brazil and their willingness to help me put together all the pieces of the Elite jig-saw puzzle, including the identification and marketing of sponsorships for the Ellus Looking—"Look of the Year" models' contest.

After six months visiting the main advertising agencies in São Paulo and dozens of potential sponsors, Vivi introduced me to the owner of the clothing company Ellus, Nelson Alvarenga. Our first meeting was divided into two stages. It began in his office, where I presented the promotional video I had produced with images of the contest and statements from professionals in the Brazilian fashion industry; and it finished in his car, on the way from the factory to Abravest, the Brazilian textile and clothing trade association, where he was vice president at the time. When I got out of his car, I was sure I had found the ideal partner for my project. And so, we prepared a specific proposal to meet to Ellus's needs and expectations. Alvarenga soon closed the deal and signed our first partnership contract. From that moment on, I built much more than a business relationship with Casablancas and Alvarenga; I built a personal relationship. The growing success of our events and models consolidated our ties to the point where Alvarenga soon became a partner in the operation.

Over the years, I have told this story several times in interviews, in the books I write, and in the lectures I give all over Brazil. And someone always asks me, "But how was all that possible?" They seem to expect me to suddenly remove something from my shirtsleeve or to reveal some secret trump card, some secret ingredient that could explain how, going against all prognostics, against all "market logic," I had really been able to realize my dream at the young age of twenty-one. But the fact is that even if I made a list of all the factors that had contributed to the project's success, none of them would have taken me anywhere, if I hadn't listened to that intuition I had the moment I was skimming through that French magazine.

Letting the Intuition Flow

* ※ *

To improve intuition, it is first necessary to open a path for it to flow freely. This doesn't involve any type of "paranormal technique." Quite the contrary, it is all a matter of observing your everyday life and adopting some concrete measures to remove the obstacles that impede or make the flow of intuition difficult. Here are some hints to help you in this task:

Be clear about your objectives. Sometimes, what we think we want isn't what we really want. This discord can have the conscious mind work for a particular purpose, while the unconscious mind works for another—creating an incompatible energy. A typical example of this is the person who convinces himself on a rational basis to remain at a job even though deep down inside he hates what he is doing and is very unhappy at work. Consciously, he wants to keep his job. However, unconsciously, he cannot wait to just drop everything, and so, without even realizing, he ends up creating situations that could lead to his dismissal. The only way to align these forces and make them act in your favor is to be honest with yourself concerning your true desires, needs, and goals.

Learn to relax. As has already been mentioned, it is necessary to stop every once in a while to listen to your intuition. Meditation helps, but whoever doesn't feel inclined to do that can at least learn to loosen up and relax. Respect your needs by saving some time for yourself, pursue hobbies and personal interests; and that way, you will be giving more space for your inner voice to manifest itself.

Feed your intuition. The French mathematician, Henri Poincaré, once said that "inspiration only comes to the prepared mind," and one way to prepare your mind is to feed it with information. Bill Gates, as you learned from the previous chapter, is a person who values the power of intuition, and he leaves nothing up to chance. He knows a brilliant idea can emerge from anywhere as long as you look for it everywhere. In a lecture he gave for the Newspaper Association of America, Gates commented, "I read a lot of printed material. I read *The Economist* front to back. I read the *Journal,* not every articles but a lot of it, every day. I read the Sunday *New York Times.* I read most of the business magazines. I read science, *Scientific American.* At work, I read a lot of trade journals. I only get four trade journals at home, and I get about six at the office." And that list doesn't take into consideration books, online reading, and other sources of information.

Cultivate relationships. Why is it that some people are able to make precise evaluations of someone they have just met while others make imprecise evaluations? Is it because they are more intuitive? Not necessarily. It would be more correct to say they are more likely to make accurate, instinctive evaluations because they dedicate themselves to cultivating relationships. The contact, interaction, and interest they have with others make them more experienced and sensitive in dealing with other human beings. This stimulates their intuition when it comes time to formulating a first impression about someone they just met. David Funder, professor of psychology at the University of California, explains, "A good judge of personality isn't just someone who is smarter—it's someone who gets out and spends time with people."[3]

The best example of people making evaluations about someone they have just met was one I experienced personally, when I met Jack Nicklaus, considered the best golfer of the century, for the first time at the Golden Bear head offices concerning the Villa

---

[3] Go to *Psychology Today* online at http://www.psychologytoday.com/rss/pto-20040713-000004.html.

Trump golf course project. That experience is detailed in the testimonial Nicklaus wrote for my first book, *POI: The Power of
Ideas*, just minutes after we met (it is important to mention I
never played golf in my life):

> To achieve success in golf, business and life, you must
> have vision. Ricardo Bellino is a man with vision, as well
> as great enthusiasm and spirit. He understands that good
> business is born out of good ideas. Ricardo appears to
> meld motivation with visualization to achieve his desired
> success. In many ways, he approaches business like one
> might approach a golf hole—he sees his goal at one end,
> plots his strategy, visualizes the potential hazards he
> might cross, and sets forth in motion his game plan.
> Ricardo's understanding of people and how to bridge
> personalities in putting together a deal should bode well
> for him in the business world.

Chapter 4

BEYOND WORDS

* ✳ *

By failing to prepare,
you are preparing to fail.
—BENJAMIN FRANKLIN

The stopwatch has been started. You have three minutes to sell your idea and only a few seconds to make a favorable enough first impression to open the first door, the door of empathy. What do you do?

Before reading any further, try to stop a second and imagine yourself in that situation. You are face-to-face with the person who could buy your idea or not, no matter what it is: a new product, business, or your services. You could also be trying to sell the idea that you are the right person for a certain job, that you are ready to get that promotion, that you deserve a raise, that your project will benefit the company, or that your suggestion will contribute to an improvement in work conditions. The person standing in front of you looks at his watch and gives you three minutes, just like Donald Trump did to me when I first met him. Think of how you would act in this situation. What would you do? What would you say and how would you say it?

Ready?

To sell an idea in three minutes requires intuition and preparation. In the first three chapters, we spoke about intuition. In this and the following chapters, we will speak about preparation.

Before anything else, you have to get ready to make a good impression. We know that as soon as someone sets eyes on you, his or her adaptive unconscious instantly captures and processes a set of data about you. Therefore, the person begins to form a mental image about you, which may be positive or negative. This data refers to everything you transmit through your appearance, dress, posture, tone of voice, facial and body expression, gestures, etc. In other words, the greater the consciousness and control you have over these elements, the greater your chances for positively influencing the way others perceive you.

Before selling your idea, you must sell your image. Alfred Lyon, who was president of Phillip Morris in the 1940s and is considered to be one of the masters of sales in the United States, always insisted on this point. When he spoke with his sales teams, he used to emphasize, "Your clients do not buy your product. They buy you. Sell yourself first!"[4] For him, to sell yourself meant to create empathy with your audience, have the other person see you as someone reliable, interesting, pleasant, and not like someone only interested in having him pull out his checkbook.

Nowadays, no one doubts the importance of image and the need to work on it. However, to work on your image does not

---

[4] Cited in Peter Krass, *The Book of Business Wisdom*, New York: John Wiley & Sons, 1997.

mean to memorize a set of "rules," thus removing all individual-ism. Whoever does this ends up creating an artificial image that causes more aversion than affinity. Spontaneity adds a fundamental touch to your interaction with others, because it transmits the feeling that you are being sincere. If not, your interlocutor could close up and think, "This guy memorized some line just to convince me," and it is very difficult to move forward toward success after that.

To prepare yourself means being conscious of a series of elements that are important when someone is forming a first impression about you, and knowing how to combine them with your spontaneity and your intuition at the moment. Businessman John H. Johnson, gives us a good example of how this works in practice. A grandson of slaves, born in poverty, Johnson had much to overcome in founding Johnson Publishing Company, a publisher whose main publication, *Ebony* magazine, has been around for more than sixty years and is read by approximately thirty million people every month. All along his path he faced countless obstacles, including racial prejudice. Nevertheless, he became famous for being able to sell anything to anyone in five minutes or less. "In the very beginning as a salesman, I used to ask my customers and potential customers for only five minutes of their time. In reality, I became known for asking for only two minutes," recalls the businessman in the book, *The Book of Business Wisdom*, by Peter Krass. He goes on to add, "What made these five minutes effective wasn't only the five minutes the customer was able to see, but the weeks and months of preparation that he couldn't see."

It bears repeating that to prepare yourself is to know everything you can to help you make a good impression, and, of course, to take full advantage of this. Therefore, we need to analyze the elements that come into play when two people meet for the first time.

The Body Speaks— Unmistakeably!

* ❋ *

When getting ready for your big meeting, it is not enough to know what to say. You need to know how to say it. Albert Mehrabian, a pioneer in the study of body language and a Ph.D. in psychology and Professor Emeritus at the University of California, has been studying the subject for more than forty years. He classified the elements that interact when a message is transmitted during a face-to-face conversation, and he attributed a percentage to each element related to its importance in message transmission. His classification of the three Vs of communication is as follows:

1. Verbal elements (words)—7 percent.

2. Vocal elements (tone of voice, inflection, timbre, rhythm, pause, cadence, interjections, etc.)—38 percent.

3. Visual elements (nonverbal aspects such as image and body language)—55 percent.

As surprising as it may seem, *the nonverbal elements are responsible for more than half of a verbal communication's chances for success.* Even the tone a word is spoken in exerts a bigger effect on the listener than the very meaning of the word. In other words, what is important is not only the content, but the way that content is presented. A message without great importance, transmitted by someone full of vigor and enthusiasm, is received with much greater interest than a brilliant message transmitted by a listless and boring person. A classic example of this is the poll conducted after the televised debate held in 1960 between Richard Nixon and John F. Kennedy, both candidates for president of the United States. When the poll takers asked those who had only listened to the debate on the radio, which of the two had won, the majority gave the victory to Nixon. However, when the same poll was taken with the public that watched the debate on television, the result was a overwhelming victory for Kennedy— who, as we know, ended up winning the election. It isn't hard to figure out what happened. Young, vigorous, and emitting energy from every pore, Kennedy had a much more powerful image than Nixon. Those who could only hear him gave the victory to Nixon, but those who could hear and see him, gave the victory to his opponent.

Another famous example that is now part of Hollywood's anecdote collection is about Sam Goldwyn, the legendary film producer and one of the founders of Metro Goldwyn Mayer, responsible for the production of classics such as *Ben Hur*. Goldwyn once met with a scriptwriter to listen to his ideas about a new movie. However, the scriptwriter expressed himself in such a boring manner that Goldwyn fell asleep in the middle of the meeting. The man was offended, woke up Goldwyn, and said,

"I'm asking you your opinion about my idea and you fall asleep!" To which Goldwyn replied, "And isn't falling asleep an opinion?"

Voice, Sweet Voice

* ✳ *

What makes this puzzle all the more complex is the fact that the theoretically easiest element to control—the word—is what carries the least weight in the effectiveness of the message. You can carefully rehearse your words, but how do you control the tone, rhythm, and cadence of your voice? A good start is by developing the habit of listening to yourself when you speak. We tend to automatically register the characteristics of someone who is talking to us—"Tom's always shrieking. He shouts rather than speaks, stutters, whispers, has poor diction . . . "—but we rarely do that with our own voice. It can also help if you ask another person's opinion. Many times other people point out characteristics that we don't even imagine having. Using these observations, it is possible to seek some kind of balance: not speak too loudly or too softly, not too quickly nor too slowly. If your speech rhythm is too droning, the listener will lose interest. If it is exaggeratedly emphatic, it could sound aggressive. A few interjections here and there indicate you are paying attention to what the other person is saying; too many interjections sound like nervous twitches or irritating habits. Try talking to someone who says "uh-huh" every other word and see for yourself how nerve-wracking this habit can be. A relaxed tone of voice helps break the ice; excess relaxation can be interpreted as disrespect.

And of course, since you are not talking to yourself, but to another person, it is also important to adjust the rhythm and tone of your voice to that of your audience, which means pausing at the right moment so other persons can express their opinions. Also make sure not to "run the person over" with your speech, interrupting the other person's reasoning and leaving him or her with the feeling that you are not paying the least attention to what the person is saying.

There are several aspects to be considered, and in more complex cases it may be necessary to seek specialized professional help with speech therapists or audiologists. However, developing your voice is a worthwhile investment. After all, the way your words sound is responsible for 38 percent of your message's effectiveness.

The Visual Elements

* ✳ *

If we lived in a perfect world, people wouldn't give so much importance to appearance. Everyone would try to see what the other person really is, and many more people would have the vision and perspicacity of John Casablancas, who was able to see, in that inexperienced and penniless student I once was, a person with the necessary conviction and energy to transform ideas into reality. But unfortunately, that's just not how things are. In his book, *Blink*, Malcolm Gladwell says that when he began to let his hair grow to form an Afro, he began to be stopped in traffic with much greater frequency than before, even though he continued driving the same way he always drove. He also refers to an experience in which musicians who were candidates to fill vacancies in an orchestra took their tests from behind a curtain, without the people in charge of the selection being able to see them play. The result was that people were chosen who would have normally been quickly rejected if the selection panel had the chance to evaluate them based on appearance first. You probably know countless similar stories, if you didn't personally go through one. That's why the third "V" in the equation proposed by professor Mehrabian in the "visual elements" carries so much weight, to the point of being responsible for 55 percent of the efficiency of a message transmitted during a face-to-face conversation between two people.

A former employee once told me the following story. When she was a student, she decided to increase her income and applied for a temporary position in a large department store chain. The hiring process was held in a large room with several rows of chairs arranged so that the candidates could sit down and fill out their application forms. There was a desk in the back of the room for the human resources person who was in charge of handing out the applications to the candidates as they arrived. My former employee sat in the back row and was able to observe the HR person up close. She noticed that the screener immediately told some of the people that the vacancies had already been filled and dismissed them without asking a single question. A little later, another person would arrive, and the same screener would hand them an application without any problem.

My former employee continued observing the scene and soon realized that the people being rejected all had certain characteristics in common. They were either poorly dressed, with a sloppy appearance, or to the contrary, overdressed, as if they were applying for an executive position, and not that of a sales clerk. The people in the first group presented an image that did not fit with the image the department store wanted to present to its customers. Those in the second group by their appearance suggested a certain disdain for the positions being offered, as if through their clothes they were saying, "My real job is something else, this is just a part-time activity." Of course, these impressions could have been erroneous, and it is possible that both groups contained people who could have been excellent clerks and salespeople. But the fact of the matter is the HR person had very little time to fill a large number of positions, and she couldn't take the luxury of investing in someone who right off the bat gave her the impression of not matching the position being offered by the company.

Whether we like it or not, we are constantly subjected to this type of prejudgment. Therefore, it is a simple matter of good sense to try to turn the game around in your favor. You do not need to be a fashion and style specialist to know that your clothes transmit a message about you, and that, upon deciding how to dress, you will also be deciding the message you wish to transmit.

However, your dress is only one of the visual elements that are responsible for 55 percent of your communication's effectiveness. Body language plays a decisive role, and it can confirm, emphasize, or even contradict your words. The human face has approximately eighty muscles capable of producing more than seven thousand facial expressions. And let's not forget about the rest of your body. How can you get someone excited about your ideas if you look crestfallen, with your shoulders hanging low, in a discouraged posture? Another example of poor body language is someone who maintains an impassive demeanor the entire time you are communicating, who stares at you without moving a single muscle. Even if that person is listening to every single word you say, you will have the feeling that he or she does not hear you, or has no interest in hearing you, because small yet powerful gestures of kindness and understanding, such as a compassionate look, a smile, a nod of the head, are not present. No matter how much such people insist that they are interested and have understood what you have said, you will continue to have the feeling that they didn't pay any attention. Their body language contradicts their words, and that is the impression that remains.

It may seem very commonplace to insist on the importance of a smile, but the fact is that even such an apparently insignificant detail as this can have a lot of weight, to the point of attracting science's attention. Paul Ekman, professor at the University of California's College of Medicine, is one of the most important specialists in the study of facial expressions. He was recently called by the American government to render advice on the analysis of the physiognomic traits of terrorists. According to Ekman, the smile is a sign we instinctively seek when we see a new face. "We can pick up a smile from thirty meters away. A smile lets us know that we're likely to get a positive reception, and it's hard not to reciprocate, " says the professor.[5]

---

[5] Go to http://www.true.com/magazine/dating_first_impression2.htm.

From Theory to Practice

* ✳ *

By now, you may be asking yourself how is it possible to control all these variables that influence a message's degree of effectiveness. If the facial muscles alone can produce thousands of expressions, how can we deal with all this when it comes time to sell an idea in three minutes?

The answer is a lot easier than it looks. The big secret is to have a deep and genuine conviction that your idea is really good, that it has every reason to work and become a successful business. Robert Woodruff, the man who headed Coca-Cola for more than sixty years, once said:

> No sales act is successful unless something of the salesperson is present. His personal integrity, his belief in himself and in his product must be an essential part of each sales agreement . . . The mere act of completing an exchange of goods or products for an agreed upon price does not necessarily comprise a successful sale, regardless of the profit, because the true salesperson must sell a little of himself with each sale. Furthermore, it is necessary for him to be a man who believes in himself and in his product. But that is still not all. The salesman needs to believe that what he sells will help the business of the merchant or the purchasing company.[6]

---

[6] Cited in Peter Krass (1997).

If this conviction Woodruff refers to is strong enough, it will be evident in your gestures and words, in your verbal and body language, in your smile and look, and even in your handshake. Upon sincerely believing in your idea, you literally exhale enthusiasm and infect the other person with your conviction. I had the chance to put that into practice many times.

When I went to meet with Donald Trump to sell him the Villa Trump project and he gave me those famous three minutes, my only "trump card" was my conviction that the idea would be a tremendous success. If he had a good first impression about me it was because everything about me exhaled that genuine, sincere, and deep conviction, the determination to make a dream come true. Trump describes the impression he had at our first meeting in his testimonial for my book *POI: The Power of Ideas*: "My first impression when I met Bellino was that he was a determined and well-informed person. He knows what I do; he knows the Brazilian market; he knows what's necessary to achieve the objectives in his business; in other words, he knows what he's doing," wrote the megabusinessman.

True conviction is something that cannot be faked. Unless you are a professional actor, and a very good one at that, it is extremely difficult, if not impossible, to train dozens of facial muscles to transmit certain images that do not correspond to reality: that is, pass on the enthusiasm, express a determination, or manifest a conviction you do not feel. And even worse than passing on the idea that you are discouraged or insecure is to pass on the impression you are not being sincere. In reality, depending on the person you are dealing with, even if you let a certain amount of anxiety and insecurity become evident, he or she may still have a good impression about you if in the end your enthusiasm and convictions prevail. That is what happened to me in my first meeting with John Casablancas. In his testimonial for *POI: The Power of Ideas*, he describes this episode in the following manner:

> A decisive factor to my buying into the idea of taking Elite to Brazil, in the beginning, was Bellino's persistence. Before I ever liked the idea of taking Elite to Brazil, I liked Bellino. . . . I was moved when I saw that young boy who had come from so far away and who was so excited to meet me after so many attempts. I liked his persistence and his enthusiasm. So, at that first meeting, Ricardo did not transmit any security, he was really anxious. But he did transmit a great desire to get it right, a very strong desire to achieve things, to make his idea come true. I have always been much more influenced by a person's characteristics than those things that are pre-arranged in someone's personality before the meeting. I do not get impressed with people who have the gift of words. What really impresses me in people is enthusiasm, transparency, character, willingness, desire, wanting to do things. When Bellino has an idea, he begins to squeeze it in every manner possible to see everything he can extract from it. I greatly admire his capacity to get enthused and to transform an idea into several actions. I noticed that ever since our very first meeting.

The best way to make a bad impression is to demonstrate excessive nervousness because you are concerned about making a good impression. Preparation, as I said before, cannot exclude spontaneity nor become a straightjacket of memorized words and gestures that end up creating an effect opposite to the one desired. Believe in your idea, and your entire body will express just that.

Many things changed since that first meeting with John Casablancas. With time and experience, I learned to control the anxiety and insecurity of my first years as a salesman of ideas. But the enthusiasm, determination, and willingness to make things work out, well, those have all remained the same.

Chapter 5

KNOW The PERSON
You Are TALKING TO

———— * ✳ * ————

*"All men who have turned out worth anything
have had a chief hand in their own education."*
—SIR WALTER SCOTT

The three-V formula discussed in Chapter 4 shows us that 55 percent of the effectiveness of a message transmitted in a face-to-face conversation depends on visual elements; 38 percent depends on vocal elements; and only 7 percent refers to the verbal element, or words themselves.

The Power of the Word

* ✳ *

However, these percentages can lead to a fatal error the moment you try to successfully sell your idea, and this error consists of underestimating or disdaining the power of words.

No matter how great the weight of the visual and vocal elements, if you are talking to business professionals, they will be evaluating not only how you present your talk, but also each one of the words. As they listen to you, it is almost as if they were automatically filling in a mental questionnaire. Does this person know what he is talking about? Does she go straight to the point? Is there any basis to what he is saying or is he just trying to take me for a ride? Is she getting my attention, making me want to hear more, or am I just wasting my time? Even if you have been "approved" in the other areas, this is when that 7 percent that corresponds to the role of words in the effectiveness of a message can mean the difference between success and failure.

There is an interesting example of this in the first season of the *The Apprentice*, the successful reality show hosted by Donald Trump. In one of the final episodes, there were only four candidates in the running for a $250,000-a-year job in the Trump Organization. During the show, the four candidates had eliminated the other contestants by defeating them in a series of tasks that tested their leadership capacity, their initiative, and their business talent. The next step consisted of a series of individual interviews conducted by employees who had Donald Trump's trust. Among the four finalists, there was a pretty young girl who attracted everyone's attention with her charisma and appearance, and she stood out as one of the favorites to win the competition. However, after analyzing the results from the interviews, the interviewers said the candidate was not "consistent" in her answers, and her words sounded empty. The result: despite her beauty, charisma, and strong performance in the tests, she ended up being summarily fired. In other words, all of the other elements responsible for 93 percent of the message's effectiveness were not sufficient to help her when she had to demonstrate her domination of the other 7 percent—words.

Talk is efficient when it captures the attention of the listener and arouses that person's interest. That is how you ask for three minutes of someone's time and end up getting a half hour, or more. Before founding his publishing empire, John H. Johnson worked as an insurance salesman, and he was so successful he ended up becoming senior partner at the company for which he worked, Supreme Life Insurance. Johnson explained his sales technique by saying, "Sometimes you just cannot tell your story in five minutes, but if you ask for just five minutes, people will be more likely to listen to you. If you can put your foot in the door and tell them a good story, they'll let you finish, even if it takes thirty minutes or an hour. If, on the other hand, there's no interest in what you are saying, five minutes is already too much."[7]

Nowadays, the maxim, "time is money" seems to be truer than ever, and the five minutes that Johnson used to ask for have been reduced to three—exactly the amount of time Donald Trump gave me to sell my idea. But, although people's time is getting shorter and shorter, the formula for attracting their attention and making the most of that time continues to be the same one Johnson used years ago, when he was a salesman. He describes these principles in the following manner:

1. Capture the client's attention in the first two or three seconds.

2. Find the vulnerable point. Everyone has something that will make him/her say yes.

---

[7] Cited in Peter Krass (1997).

3. Find and cultivate points in common. You and the client may disagree about several things, [but] you are not there to talk about what separates you. You are there to emphasize values, hopes, and aspirations that unite both of you.[8]

I would not be able to describe, word for word, what I told Donald Trump during those three minutes. After all, I didn't use any memorized talk that could be reproduced automatically later on, and that wouldn't matter anyway. I was selling him the idea for Villa Trump, and you would be selling something else. But I can certainly say that I used all three principles cited by Johnson. And I can also say that if part of the secret to grabbing someone's attention is finding their vulnerable point and aspects you have in common, another part consists of knowing both your idea and the person to whom you are selling it.

To know your idea well means you have explored it enough to know its feasibility, its breakdown, and its means for implementation. It means that you have a consistent project and you are capable of presenting it in a concise way, to supply any information that is requested, and to defend it with confidence against any objections that may arise. In other words, you are sure your idea works and you are prepared to show why.

The idea of building Villa Trump—which will be the largest and most exclusive golf condo in Latin America and the first enterprise with Trump's brand in Brazil—emerged from an intuition I had during a conversation with a neighbor. This neigh-

---

[8] Cited in Peter Krass, *The Book of Business Wisdom*. New York: John Wiley, 1997.

bor, who works in real estate, asked me one evening if I knew of anyone interested in buying a large tract of land that was for sale in the area near Itatiba, in the State of São Paulo. When I heard him, I had a "snap" thought. "Wait a second, if this area is as fantastic as you are telling me, with an excellent location, then let's create the first Donald Trump enterprise in Brazil." My neighbor told me to cut it out, to quit the "crazy talk," because all he wanted to do was sell that land. So, I answered him immediately, "Look, I already see this as a done deal."

I kept the material about the land and at that same moment called an Argentine friend of mine living in Miami who takes care of everything involving the image, logos, and visual presentations for my company. I told him I needed to create a presentation for the Villa Trump Project and I explained the idea to him. In a matter of hours, he sent me a logo proposal, with images of golf courses and the entire visual concept already created. It was all very beautiful, but, until that moment, it was all just a concept with beautiful images. It was necessary to develop quality content, something that would show Trump that the idea had potential to become a profitable business. That's why Samuel Goldstein, my partner, and I dug deep into the presentation, developing all the components necessary to define the project in marketing terms, including some preliminary studies related to economic feasibility. I sent the material to Trump together with a cover letter written by John Casablancas, my partner in implementing the Elite modeling agency in Brazil.

Some time later, I was at the house of my neighbor who had brought me the proposal to sell the land, when my mobile phone rang. To my great surprise, it was Donald Trump's secretary asking if I would be available to talk with him at that exact moment.

Trump came to the phone to congratulate me for the letter Casablancas had sent him, for the credit I had earned with the founder of Elite, and also for my idea. So, I asked him what he thought about the presentation I had sent. To my great surprise, he said he hadn't even read the presentation: Casablancas' letter had been enough to motivate him to get in touch with me. Trump asked me to send him the material again; as soon as he received it, he called me again, this time asking me to schedule an appointment with his secretary for the next week.

It is difficult to describe the euphoria I felt. However, this inebriating feeling did not affect my good sense. I knew that as much as Trump had liked my idea, the deal would only be closed if the project was sufficiently consistent to convince him that the idea had reason to work. Samuel and I rolled up our sleeves and got to work. I had to know the cost of the land, of the golf course projects, of the urbanization and infrastructure, of the clubs and residences, in short, of everything that involved Villa Trump. We worked around the clock talking to specialists from all areas, making calculations, budgets, and estimates, exploring all possibilities, examining every detail. Armed with all this, I prepared to meet with Donald Trump. In the testimonial he wrote for my book *POI: The Power of Ideas*, Trump commented, "Concerning Villa Trump, the decisive factor for me to buy into the idea was that it really was good. Bellino had analyzed the project in depth and I noticed it had every reason to work. Villa Trump will be a big success because of all of this."

Now we get to the other part of the equation: knowing as well as you can the person you are trying to sell something to. All the effort I had put into the presentation wouldn't have gotten me anywhere if the whole idea hadn't caught Trump's interest. I could never have made the idea interest him if I didn't know beforehand what his interests were. I didn't make use of any fortune-telling method. Quite the contrary, it was all a matter of work: that is, making the effort to gather information, to research, to get informed about his style, his personality, his likes, and his way of thinking and acting. It is a mistake to think that the possibility of profit alone is sufficient to motivate a businessman to consider the proposal of a young businessman he didn't know and to embark on a commercial adventure in a country he also didn't know. As I wrote in my book, *Stone Soup: Ten Ingredients for You to Create Your Recipe to Success:*

> Before mentioning the benefits the idea will bring, it is necessary to know which benefits your investor candidate expects. . . . Of course the financial return is important. But it may not be enough to close a deal. A series of factors come into play: the return in terms of prestige, reputation, projection, personal satisfaction—what could be better than to make money with a project and to top it off, have the pleasure of participating in it?

However, studying someone's habits and preferences will not help you if you do not know how to complement this information with your intuition, with your feeling. When the final presentation for Villa Trump was ready, I presented it to several specialists and consultants so they could give me their opinions. They were all unanimous in affirming it was necessary to "streamline" the material, eliminating a good part of the information that referred to marketing. "Trump is interested in numbers. Be more objective," they told me. But I refused to summarize the presentation.

"Trump is synonymous with marketing," I insisted. "Money isn't the most important thing for him today. Of course, he doesn't want to lose money. But to be part of a business with appeal, capable of even further leveraging his brand, that is fundamental." To the great horror and dismay of our consultants, everything they wanted to eliminate was maintained. And the fact is that was exactly what made Trump become enchanted with the presentation and close the deal. If I had agreed to exclude all of that and ignored my intuition and the information I had about Donald Trump's personality and style, it would have been highly unlikely that the idea would have caught his interest to the point of his closing the deal after the famous three minutes.

Instead of a Network, Create a Brotherhood

* ※ *

One factor of great importance in selling my idea to Donald Trump was the cover letter written by John Casablancas. You may think, "It's easy that way. If I knew someone who could open the doors, even I would have been successful!" My reply to that is: Get busy and cultivate friendships and expand your circle of relationships. Thinking things were easy for me because of John Casablancas' cover letter is an illusion. First, because when I met Casablancas there was no one to introduce me to him. It took a tremendous effort on my part to overcome insecurities such as, "Why would such an important person talk to an unknown student without a penny to his name?" And I also had to make use of a huge dose of persistence for that first contact to happen. Second, it is important to underscore that after the Brazilian Elite agency took off we didn't remain friends by chance. The friendship that emerged between us was cultivated and based on the mutual respect and ethics that have always guided my professional career. That's why it survived the most adverse circumstances that so often bury even the most solid friendships. And that's how we remained friends even after the failure of some of our joint initiatives. Therefore, when the creator of Elite Models agreed to write a cover letter to Donald Trump, that decision was not the fruit of a moment, but of eighteen years of friendship.

It is fashionable nowadays to talk about the creation of networks, or relationship networks. There are many books and courses that underscore the advantages you gain from a professional point of view by expanding your list of contacts and relations. And these advantages are frequently summarized into one: gain access to people who can somehow help you reach your objectives. It just so happens that this is a very limited view of a relationship network, because it transforms human relations into a mere exchange of favors. This may work, but only to a certain point. Since in this case there are no true ties between the people, only interests, as soon as a person is no longer "useful," he is automatically discarded—and that ends up being the fate of those who concern themselves with making "contacts" instead of friends.

The true network is more like a brotherhood than a list of contacts. People in a brotherhood are driven by the healthy and natural interest of making friends, exchanging experiences, and learning from peers. When properly nurtured, these ties become a network of mutual support that is essential not only for our professional lives but for our personal lives as well. What truly matters here is not to think about whom you can "use," but on whom you can count.

Social Intelligence

* ❋ *

It is this broader view of human relationships that constitutes *social intelligence,* which Edward Thorndike, the great American educator and psychologist, defined as the skill each individual uses to understand and deal with other people. Social intelligence is fundamental for anyone who hopes to be successful in the corporate environment.

Lee Iacocca, the renowned executive who reinvented Chrysler, used to say, "After all, business is nothing but a bunch of human relationships." That is the typical point of view of a person equipped with a high level of social intelligence, which, most certainly, contributed to Iacocca's becoming one of the living legends of the business world. Knowing how to relate with people implies, among other things, knowing how to listen to them and respect them, and not use them as a target for your ill humor or frustrations. Let the moment of anger or irritation pass. Actually, to think before speaking or acting, or as it is more popularly called, to "chill out," is one of those characteristics that identifies someone's "social competence," or level of social intelligence.

Several studies on the topic point out the different aspects that characterize the individual with a high level of social intelligence. But that which science points out, practice confirms. After all, the characteristics listed below appear frequently in the biographies of successful people—in business and in life.

Accept others as they are. In social life, nothing is more wearing than trying to change people or shape them according to our likes and needs. Besides being useless, these attempts make you appear intolerant or manipulative. Rather than trying to force others to be what they are not, a person with social intelligence is concerned with trying to find out how people can contribute, while remaining as they are.

Admit your errors. From a social point of view, few "pests" are worse than those who are always right. Those who never admit their own errors end up scaring off others or oppressing them with their arrogance. A little humility makes people seem more human and accessible, basic requirements for a healthy relationship.

Demonstrate curiosity and interest in people and the world in general. No one with a "one-track mind," who can only talk about a specific subject—about work for example—is able to form a broad circle of friends. The "boring" label follows those people everywhere, and most of the time, they are limited to superficial relationships with other people just like them.

Be socially aware. This is a natural spin-off from the genuine interest for people that characterizes someone equipped with social intelligence. This type of person is not indifferent to society's problems, and whenever possible, he or she does not refuse to intervene to help solve these problems.

Be punctual. This seems like an insignificant detail, but it's not. Not making other people wait unnecessarily is a sign of respect and consideration.

Be sensitive to the needs and desires of others. A socially intelligent person is someone who knows how to make others feel like they are being understood, that they are worthy of attention. And this occurs as a result of the person's sensitivity with regard to the yearnings of those around him. This is an indispensable characteristic to deal with egos, interests, and vanities—things never lacking in a group of interacting humans, whether in business or among family members and friends.

Make fair judgments; be honest with yourself and with others. There is no bigger misunderstanding than to confuse flattery with social intelligence. People with this type of intelligence do not flatter nor do they like being flattered. Instead, they give their opinions honestly—whether those opinions are constructive criticism or praise—and they try to listen to all parties involved before reaching a conclusion.

Know how to transmit relevant information and to distinguish what is relevant in the information you receive. Idle chatter is not a sign of elevated social intelligence—nor is giving everything you hear the same weight. In reality, the lack of objectivity and coherence when transmitting information and the lack of discernment when retaining and reproducing it indicate a low level of social intelligence.

Know how to put yourself in someone else's shoes. This is an essential characteristic for creating empathy. It is not merely a question of listening to the other person, but of listening in an understanding manner, to the point of imagining yourself in the other person's shoes.

Have a good memory for names, faces, and facts. A person with good social intelligence calls others by their name—including the superintendent of the building, the assistant at the company, the waiter at the restaurant, and the man at the hot dog stand. People with social intelligence always ask how you are doing when they see you even though they are not part of your intimate circle of friends. If, for example, you should say your mother is ill, you can be sure that when you see that person again, even if it is a month later, he or she will ask you, "How is your mother feeling?"

Be able to engage in conversations with different types of people. It does not matter if she is the cleaning woman at your house, the director of your company, your best friend, or a complete stranger. A socially intelligent person knows how to deal with differences and always finds and delves into points in common.

Adapt well in social situations. Do you know that person who always stands in the corner at parties? The person who always looks completely out of place at meetings? The only person who appears to be ill at ease, uncomfortable, upset? That is a person who needs to improve his or her social intelligence.

Have good humor. Know how to laugh about yourself, face life in a positive manner, and have the good sense to notice that others are not to blame if you crashed your car, if your business dealings did not go as expected, or if it rained the day you decided to go to the beach. All of this demonstrates your competence at creating and cultivating good relationships.

Know the rules and norms that govern human relations. This characteristic includes all the others, and more: gestures of courtesy; signs of good will and receptivity; social etiquette; words and behaviors fitting the person, the occasion, and the degree of intimacy you have with the other; respect for ethnic and cultural differences; and so on. There is no complete list. Instead, we learn as we leave.

Chapter 6

MIDAS
And
SADIM

———— * ✳ * ————

*"The majority of men meet with
failure because of their lack of persistence
in creating new plans to take
the place of those which fail."*
—NAPOLEON HILL

Specialists in selling ideas in three minutes are people who
have developed their "Midas touch." This expression stems
from the age-old Greek legend according to which the god
Dionysius decided to reward Midas, the King of Phrygia, for
having offered shelter and protection to his old tutor when the
latter found himself in a very difficult situation. As his reward,
Midas asked for the gift of transforming everything he touched
into gold. He later begged the god to free him from that power,
because even food was being transformed into gold upon touch-

ing his lips. Thus, even with all the gold he could ever wish for, he was on the verge of starvation.

However, contrary to the legend from which the expression is derived, the Midas touch does not refer to a divine blessing or to a curse. It refers to the ability some people have to obtain profits where others only find losses, of finding opportunities where no one else sees them, of transforming ideas into successful businesses. Just as Midas transformed everything into gold, people with the Midas touch change everything they put their hands on for the better. If the company is going bankrupt, they recover it; if the business is sinking, they make it prosper; if the project cannot get off the drawing board, they put it into practice; if discouragement runs rampant, they restore enthusiasm; if arguing and disagreements prevail, they establish a cooperative environment.

There are countless examples of people with the Midas touch. Sílvio Santos took over a business riddled with debt that operated in the basement of a building and transformed it into the Baú da Felicidade, a business that is still one of his Brazilian primary enterprises. Starting with a hospital on the verge of bankruptcy, Edson de Godoy Bueno created Amil, the most successful health plan company in Brazil. In the middle of the fuel crisis of the 1970s, Salim Mattar did what no one would have ever dreamed of doing at that time: he opened a car rental company, Localiza, which would eventually become one of the largest in Brazil. There are many stories, and they involve famous and other not-so-famous people. But they all prospered because of their Midas touch. You probably know many of them: that employee who seems to have a solution for everything and who has a meteoric rise in the company; the salesman who can sell a refrigerator to an Eskimo; the businessman who was successful in using an idea no one believed in, and many more.

However, if everyone has heard of the Midas touch, not everyone has heard of his opposite, King Sadim. They may not know him, but they most assuredly have seen him in action. Sadim is Midas written backwards. And just as his name indicates, he is the opposite of Midas. If the king of Phrygia transformed everything into gold, King Sadim has the power to deteriorate everything he touches. If the business is profitable, he is able to make it lose money; if the idea is good, he is able to ruin it; if there is friendship and cooperation, he quickly installs distrust and discord. King Sadim is an extremely insecure person with very low self-esteem. However, since he is unable to work out his weak points, because he does not even admit to having any, he uses arrogance to hide them even from himself. King Sadim never recognizes himself as such. He believes he is a Midas, though the results of his actions are always there to unmask him. But of course, that does not stop him. Sadim is a master at blaming others for his own blindness and incompetence, and he believes piously in the fantasies he invents to disguise his failures. And he moves forward, dauntless, unaware of the path of destruction he leaves behind.

Unfortunately, sooner or later it is inevitable that we cross paths with a Sadim, whether in our professional or personal lives. And knowing how to recognize him, as well as knowing the weapons he uses and learning how to neutralize them, is a matter of survival.

Identifying Sadim

* ✳ *

Every human being is a complex mixture of emotions and feelings, a combination of positive and not-so-positive elements, and King Sadim is no exception. It just so happens that his feelings of inferiority and inadequacy are so deep, and his refusal to admit this is so powerful, that he ends up being driven by an uncontrollable impulse to project onto others those characteristics he cannot recognize in himself. That is the only way he knows to make himself feel a little better. This behavior makes him seem almost like a caricature of human arrogance at its most extreme. In him, arrogance, pettiness, and egoism are clearly evident without any filter, because self-criticism, equilibrium, and good sense cannot be cultivated by a person who refuses to see his own faults. That is why it is easy to observe the following elements in King Sadim:

The magic mirror Just like the evil step-mother in the story of Snow White, King Sadim also has a special mirror which only shows what he wants to see. Because of this distortion, he sees his arrogance as magnanimity, his pettiness as generosity, his rancor as "justice," his incompetence as "the others' fault," and so on.

The court jester For the magic mirror to be even more effective, King Sadim tries to surround himself with a retinue of flatterers whose competence is measured by their ability to ingratiate themselves. If you have ever had a King Sadim as a boss, you must have noticed that he always places members of his retinue in key positions, even at the expense of the company's health and profitability. Of course he will say that his choices are based on competence, but anyone (except for him) can see that the main, if not the only, criterion is to strengthen his position and his ego. The flatterers never question or challenge his "competence" because that is something they too do not have. Surrounding himself with people that are at least as mediocre as he helps to increase his illusion of superiority.

False modesty Although he loves all the flattery, King Sadim often seeks to maintain a façade of false modesty. But this false modesty disappears the moment he thinks he is not receiving the attention he deserves. Then he screams, throws a tantrum, intimidates, threatens, maligns—all as he claims to be the target of "injustice."

Shortcuts If king Sadim is so incompetent, how is it that we so often see him in prominent positions? First, because Sadim is also a flatterer and he knows how to approach and take advantage of other Sadims who are more powerful than he. But flattery is not his only shortcut. In some cases, he can get there through a marriage of convenience or sheer luck.

The double-crosser Sometimes, people who seem to be our friends turn out later to be true Sadims. This is because dissimulation is another one of his characteristics. He can feign friendship to hitch a ride on someone's success, but sooner or later, he will try to claim this success for himself. That is when Sadim shows his true colors.

Selective memory King Sadim has the incredible gift of being able to rewrite history in his own words. Of course, he believes he is Solomon himself when it comes to justice, and he loves to say, "I am a fair person!" But in reality, words such as recognition and gratitude do not exist in his vocabulary. When he talks about the past, he always increases his own importance and reduces or eliminates the importance of others. He can actually go to the point of claiming authorship for an idea he did not have or of an initiative he did not take.

Envy Every Sadim is envious by nature. His self-esteem problems lead him to covet what others have instead of trying to obtain those things through personal effort. He not only envies wealth and power, but also anything that makes a person stand out: talents, skills, merits. He envies the fact that someone can be esteemed by others, the friends another person has, and even someone's "luck." Past achievements, academic feats, good humor, someone's family life, anything can become a reason for envy.

Personal dictionary Sadim has his own dictionary in which words take on the meaning he wants to give them. The talents of others he calls "luck" or "nepotism." His own lack of tact and social intelligence receives the name of "honesty," and in general, it is accompanied with "I tell the truth, regardless of whom it hurts." The more skillful are called "mediocre," and the more competent are always "incompetent."

The walking metamorphosis A true Sadim is always changing his mind to go along with what is fashionable or to try to contaminate others with his own eternal insecurity. If one moment he says he liked your work, the very next he may say everything you do is worthless. If today he defends a theory to the very end, tomorrow he may defend something completely different. Do not try to understand him. The best thing to do is to slip away and pretend you did not hear anything.

Rancor King Sadim is capable of remembering his classmate in elementary school who got the best grades and attracted everyone's attention—and still have feelings of hatred and resentment for that person. And if he forgets the person who helped him, he never forgets the person he believes offended him. And he will not miss the chance to seek revenge and unleash his rancor.

Paranoia A "pathologic" Sadim, in time, falls into paranoia. The insecurity he tries to hide or ignore grows in the shadows and makes him see "conspiracies" everywhere, people trying to "pull the rug from under him." Anyone who does not belong to the group of flatterers can be seen as a "traitor," and sometimes, even some of the flatterers pay the price. Since his attitudes lead to catastrophe, the clearer the signs of this catastrophe become, the greater his need to find scapegoats. His deliriums take the form of witch hunts. If something goes wrong, it is because the "conspirators" are trying to sabotage his plans, which were always so perfect. King Sadim believes the world revolves around him and everyone else's main concern is to find a way to oust him.

Sadim's Arsenal

* ** *

King Sadim does not hesitate to play dirty to reach his objectives. Watch out for the main weapons he tends to use:

Dissimulation Although he likes to appear courageous, it is nothing but bravado. In reality, he is a coward. He wants to see all hell let loose, but he does not want to be pointed out as the one who started it. So, he resorts to disguise. His attacks are almost always indirect. He tends to rely on his retinue of flatterers to do the dirty work for him, and he only attacks directly when the victim has already been wounded and has no chance to react at the time.

Sadism Like all envious people, King Sadim loves to see the object of his envy going through difficulties, and he does not waste the chance to increase other people's affliction. Anyone who has had a Sadim as a boss or collegue has already gone through this. He approaches, places his hand on your shoulder and says, "I heard that someone upstairs wants your head. Be careful, they've got their eye out for you," and then he smiles inside as he watches the victim squirm.

Disdain In the fable about the fox and the grapes, the fox cannot reach the grapes he yearns for, so he pretends to have no interest in them at all. He says, "I don't want those. They're too green." King Sadim does exactly the same thing, or worse. To reinforce his disdain, he tends to also resort to contempt, sarcasm, and derision, making every effort to make that which he envies look ridiculous.

Gossip, rumors, defamation, and slander These are some of his favorite weapons. He has a master's and a doctorate in the art of beginning and propagating gossip and rumors against his enemies, i.e., those he envies. And thus, he creates the perfect environment to use his next weapons, defamation and slander. This is all well wrapped in dissimulation. He always begins by saying, "I don't know if I should tell you, but since you're my friend . . . " or "I don't want to get involved with this, but you should know that . . . " and a series of other similar lines. King Sadim knows very well that unfounded rumors can jeopardize someone's career, because they make many people think that where there is smoke, there is fire. In reality, the correct way to think would be: where there is smoke, there is probably a Sadim starting a fire.

Scheming King Sadim is a specialist in pitting one person against another, undoing friendships, and spreading discord. Relationships are a particularly sensitive point for him. Since he is unable to maintain any kind of healthy relationship, he gets bent out of shape when he sees sincere affection between two people, or the trust a boss demonstrates toward an employee. And he will do whatever he can to pull the rug out from under his victims. And of course, all this is in the name of his "truth" and his "justice."

Embezzlement Be very careful when exposing an idea or a project to King Sadim. Thanks to his selective memory, he will feel no qualms about embezzling it and presenting it as if it were his own. Also be careful about asking him for help, even if you just want a simple suggestion. Sadim may take advantage of the situation to later say he did all the work for you.

The Antidotes for Sadim

* ✳ *

I have run into many Sadims in my lifetime. In reality, at every stage of implementation of my ideas, I've run into several of them. Some pretended to be my friend and then suddenly showed their true colors; others acted like true Sadims from the very beginning. The fact is that these characters are unavoidable. All you need is to be successful in something and they come running. What is avoidable is the mess they can make of your life or career.

What Sadim wants most is to reproduce himself and make you a Sadim as well. And this happens whenever one of his victims feels driven into a corner and ends up using the same weapons he uses: irritable reactions, pettiness, and the desire to get even at whatever cost. The popular saying is that the best revenge is to live well, and that is the ideal weapon to neutralize Sadim and not be contaminated by him. No matter how often the Sadims got in my way, I was never detained by them;

I never stopped pursuing my dreams; I never abandoned my values, nor did I ever let my good humor, my enthusiasm, and my positive manner be deteriorated by the malice and pettiness of these crownless kings.

In my book *POI: The Power of Ideas* (2003), the testimonial written by Jack Nicklaus, considered to be the best golfer of all times, contains a true antidote against the Sadims in life. Nicklaus wrote:

I am proud to say I never wished for an opponent to miss a drive or a putt in any moment in all the years I competed playing golf. Quite the contrary, I preferred to concentrate exclusively on making my best effort to do what I needed to win. This allowed me to live very comfortably with myself, regardless of the result. Furthermore, I never saw nor heard a really good player cheer for his opponent to miss, especially in professional tournaments. There are many reasons for this to be extremely rare if it ever happens: first of all, there is the natural camaraderie of golf. The best players in all phases of the game, professional and amateur, are certainly trying to do their best to beat the others at all times. But they also need to live with the others while doing this and this produces a bond among them that seems to overcome even the darkest sides of the most competitive personalities. When you experience that, when you know what its like to play badly and lose, you are not encouraged to wish that pain on another person. Although he may not be a friend in the full sense of the word, he is at least a person who shares the same experiences and challenges as you.

From this quote you get an idea why Nicklaus is such an admired and esteemed person on and off the links. It is a pity that the Sadims cannot learn anything from his words, since they do not have the humility to recognize they have something to learn. But *we* can. To not wish something bad on someone, to not hope your opponent will make a mistake during a competition, contributes to the creation of an environment of fellowship capable of withstanding all of Sadim's attacks.

Another way to immunize yourself against Sadim's arsenal is by taking care of your reputation. The more solid your credibility, the more difficult it will be for Sadim to try to discredit you using gossip and rumors. On the other hand, if he can find the slightest opening, he will do everything in his power to turn it into an enormous hole.

In conclusion, remember that Sadim should not be feared, for fear will only serve to give this buffoon an illusion of power. Nor should he be hated, because hatred deprives the hater of a valuable energy that should be used toward more useful objectives. The wisest attitude is to simply ignore him and move forward. With regard to the troubles he may cause, do not see them as obstacles, but as stimuli to send you onto even higher pursuits. As the Italian writer, Giovanni Papini, once wrote:

The best revenge against those who intend to discredit me is to seek higher pursuits. And I may not have gone so high if it had not been for those who wanted to shoot me down. The truly wise person does more: he uses the defamation thrown on him to touch up his portrait and eliminate the shadows that affect his light. The envious end up unwillingly collaborating toward his perfection.

Chapter 7

LESSONS
From
The APPRENTICE

✳ ✳ ✳

"Creativity is when
originality defeats habit."
—GEORGE LOUIS,
musician, educator, and author

You have probably already heard of the reality show called *The Apprentice*, the program on which Donald Trump, with the support of two of his closest and most experienced collaborators, George Ross and Carolyn Kepcher, challenge 16 candidates to a series of tasks designed to evaluate their potential as businesspeople. At the end of each task, the losers meet with Trump in the meeting room to discuss the reasons for their failure. The candidate who had the worst performance is eliminated from the program and hears Trump say that renowned and feared sentence, "You're fired!" And the show continues with new tasks in every episode, until in the end, only one candidate remains. The lucky winner gets a one-year work contract to preside over one of the companies in the Trump Organization.

Ever since the first episode, the show has been a tremendous success, and it is easy to see why. Throughout the reality show, the audience has the rare opportunity to witness the disputes, decisions, strategies, errors, and right moves of people who are seeking success in the business world. The meanderings of this process, which normally take place behind closed doors, are exposed in an unprecedented manner on your TV screen. It is not only entertainment, but an apprenticeship as well. Episode after episode, the candidates have to sell their image and their ideas to a demanding buyer, Donald Trump himself, a man whose intuition, experience, and talent for business have made him not only a successful businessman, but a billionaire as well.

Because I consider myself to be an eternal apprentice, it was a great honor to read the following passage in Trump's book *How to Get Rich:*

> I went back to the office in the morning to meet with George Ross. We discussed the details of the tumultuous resolution of the previous evening's task. Minutes and seconds counted, whether in the Olympics or in business. George cited a story from that morning's *New York Times* about my Brazilian partner, Ricardo Bellino, in which Ricardo said I gave him exactly three minutes to sell me his idea in January of 2003. We have been partners ever since. Ever since, we have been in business together and he just might be able to get *The Apprentice* broadcast in Brazil in the near future. He is a good exam-

ple for those who aspire to be apprentices about the value
of time. [9]

Indeed, I did participate in making the Brazilian version of *The
Apprentice* possible even without any commercial interest in the
project. In an initiative together with the People + Arts cable television network, I organized a press conference with George Ross
in Brazil to promote the launching of the program. I was
extremely satisfied when I learned that Roberto Justus, CEO for
the NewCom Group, the largest advertising group in the country,
had been chosen to host the Brazilian version of the reality show.
I had the idea that Justus should put his own stamp on the program. This perception proved successful when I watched the first
episode of the Brazilian *The Apprentice* with him. Justus's performance exceeded all expectations.

About my participation in making the reality show possible
in Brazil, Justus made the following comment:

> Ricardo Bellino is one of the most creative and enterpris-
> ing people I have ever met. Besides that he is detail ori-
> ented and everything he does is very well done . . . My
> experience with him on *The Apprentice* is further proof of
> my opinion. I asked him to articulate a meeting with
> Donald Trump to kick off the Brazilian program with
> the press. He immediately coordinated all the details,
> made the appointment and accompanied me to be sure
> everything would go as planned. In the end, as an addi-
> tional bonus, he was even able to arrange our visit to the

---

[9] Donald J. Trump, *How to Get Rich* (New York: Random House, 2004).

studios for the American program installed on the ground floor of the Trump Tower on Fifth Avenue. Together, we exchanged some good ideas about some of the tasks for the episode that involved the holding of the Trump Open—the largest golf tournament in Brazil and the production of a super show with Margarthe Menezes, both to be held in Sauípe in the state of Bahia. Ricardo also organized the award for the winning team of that episode, with a visit to the Trump Organization offices and a conversation with Donald Trump himself. It is important to underscore that what most caught my attention in this experience with Bellino was the fact that he did not want any credit whatsoever for the initiative.[10]

My involvement with the program was mainly guided by my interest in promoting the lessons the entrepreneurship show conveys, in a way never seen before, which are fundamental for anyone who yearns for professional success. In a hard-fought battle that perfectly mirrors the competition we face in real life, it is intuition and good sense that separate the losers from the winners in each task.

From the experiences of the candidates on *The Apprentice* and from the observations made by them at the American Management Association Apprentice forums and at the official site of the American reality show, I have extracted the following guidelines that can be very useful in your day-to-day life as an entrepreneur.

---

[10] As cited by Ricardo Bellino (2005).

Conduct a Productive Brainstorming Session

* ✳ *

In several *Apprentice* episodes, we saw the candidates trying to hold a brainstorming session without much success. The problem, which often occurs in many companies, is that the participants frequently deviated from the objective of the brainstorming session, which is to bring creative ideas to the surface, and got lost in meaningless discussions. Brainstorming is an essential part of the thinking process for a business or a new idea in any organization. When properly executed, it can lead to a dynamic and valuable exchange of ideas and initiatives. However, when poorly conducted, it can promote resentment and internal tension and be counterproductive.

All of the participants in a brainstorming session need to remember at every moment that nothing being discussed or criticized in these meetings is personal in nature. It is only business. Here are some of the important rules to observe for conducting a creative and successful brainstorming session:

Establish the role of leader. The leader has to act as a facilitator, monitoring the flow of ideas, and ensure that everyone has the chance to speak, that there are no interruptions, and that the discussion does not lose its predetermined focus. The leader should encourage challenge and debate among the participants, which makes the session very productive. Hostility is not healthy and should be avoided at all costs.

Define the task and maintain control. All group members should clearly understand the final objective of the business at hand. Before solutions are suggested, the available facts as well as the challenges should be reviewed and discussed.

Announce the session's objective. The path for the brainstorming session must be completely unobstructed. The purpose is to generate ideas without considering their merit at first.

Create a positive environment. The participants must feel free to be open and honest. The choice of a neutral environment is necessary. Find a room where team members can be outside of their territories, provide them with water and juices, and get to work.

Use a flipchart. This allows the group members to visualize the ideas and then discuss those that most interest them.

Encourage the flow of ideas. There should not be any rash evaluations during brainstorming. Members should not immediately seek "the idea." The team's objective is to generate several ideas. The solution will arise, almost always, from the junction of the various alternatives presented.

Carefully monitor verbal and nonverbal communication. Listen to all of the members of the group. Also pay attention to nonverbal communication: more than words, it will indicate how the participants feel in relation to the group's progress.

Periodically evaluate the group's progress. If the ideas presented do not cause enthusiasm, it is necessary to review them.

First, focus the discussion on the positive aspects of each idea. Then, focus on the negative points.

Choose the most appropriate idea for the proposed objective. During the elimination process, identify the best ideas and make a final choice. Choose an idea that is completely in line with the task's objective and that all team members are willing to support.

Make the Right Decision

* ✳ *

It is inevitable. At the end of every episode of *The Apprentice*, the losing team's project manager has to explain to Donald Trump why he made decisions that led his group to failure. As in real life, he is held responsible for the team's decisions, and he runs the serious risk of being fired when these decisions prove erroneous. In the business world, everything revolves around decisions, whether they are made by you individually, as a member of a group, or as a leader. There are decisions that have the luxury of time, such as marketing plans and budgets; others are practically "thrown" upon you and must be made that very minute. However, each of them is vital for your business or career.

Therefore, take note of these observations:

Combine intuition with strategy. Equilibrium is fundamental. Avoid the labels of "indecisive" and "impulsive." Before deciding, also evaluate the information brought by others. If the others feel they are not being considered they will undermine your support base. Refute unusable suggestions with firm and convincing arguments; otherwise, your authority will be weakened.

Make decisions for the appropriate reasons. If you are in a position of authority, make sure that your new decisions do not compromise your power. Do not underestimate yourself or your team by using simple bravado. Avoid inconsequent decisions that will only serve to create false moments of glory.

Prevention is the best medicine. Visualize the worst possible scenario that could result from your decision and be sure the risk is worthwhile.

Compensate your biased attitudes by making decisions. Are you a person who is "limited" to numbers or are you someone who looks for a greater context? Do you seek quick or long-term solutions? Improve the quality of your decisions by improving your understanding of yourself.

Practice the 80/20 rule. Recognize that 80 percent of the information you need to make a good decision can generally be gathered in a relatively short period of time. Do not wait for the remaining 20 percent. In most cases, it will probably not change the situation.

Trust in your ability to make decisions. We learn by doing. The more decisions you make, the better your chances are to learn and get it right more often. Most professional decisions do not require Solomon's wisdom, but they do require you to weigh the facts and understand the individuals involved. Upon making a bad decision, you must be flexible enough to change direction.

Pay Attention to Finances

* ✳ *

In almost every episode of *The Apprentice*, the participants have to control finances. If they receive funds to acquire material and sell lemonade in the streets of New York, they need to make enough to recover the investment and make a profit. If the task is to remodel and rent an apartment, the value of the rent should be greater than what was charged before the remodeling. Obviously, this is the basic principle for any successful business. There is no way to prosper by spending more than you earn. But dealing with finances is very complex. In today's uncertain times, in which every executive is held responsible for results, you must possess or develop a special understanding of finances. You must know how to justify a request, quantify the contributions to the company, and immediately avoid any possible unprofitability. It doesn't matter how effective your management style may be, or how innovative your ideas are, your performance will be measured dollar by dollar and cent by cent. Here are some guides:

Pay attention to the business plan. Your budget is your business plan and it should reflect everything you intend to do. If the numbers do not balance, it may not be a budget problem. You had better reexamine your business plan.

Create a contingency fund. Admit that the unforeseen happens. Anything can cost more than you expect. Last-minute deliveries, for example, can run many budgets off track.

Document everything. It is ideal to have all information concerning costs and possible alternatives in writing. Keep detailed notes about your estimates, reasoning, and calculations that made you get to those numbers.

Know your costs. Do not guess. If you do not have any way to obtain precise information, it is always best to overestimate spending and underestimate revenue.

Continuously monitor real spending versus foreseen costs in the budget. The cost of an invoice should never be a surprise. If expenses are higher than foreseen, do not put your head on the pillow and expect things to naturally get better. Take immediate initiatives. Cut expenses until you are sure the budget is back on track.

Establish checks and balances. Define limits for the expenses of different collaborators and specific tasks. Ask for prior approval or signatures for all exceptions, thus avoiding possible surprises.

Do not keep people in the dark. Continuously communicate your budget's situation to all interested parties. This is the best way to avoid unnecessary restraints.

Preserve Your Credibility

* ✳ *

The culminating point in each episode of *The Apprentice* is the moment when the losing team members are called into the meeting room to account for their loss. At that moment, the TV audience already imagines who will be attacked and criticized by their colleagues. It is almost always the people whose attitudes and behaviors have hurt their credibility in the eyes of their peers. Respect, confidence, and credibility are the intangible elements that can build or destroy a career. Gaining respect and developing credibility and confidence are critical factors for success. Effective leaders do not need to impose or demand respect—their actions earn it.

To be respected and to preserve your credibility, you should:

Create a vision. And find the key resources to make it happen.

Communicate the vision. Speak about it with confidence and consistency at every opportunity.

Be passionate. Your enthusiasm will encourage people to accept your ideas and follow your objectives. You cannot capture people's interest if you are not enthusiastic.

Be visible. Always be involved. The members of your team want a leader in the trenches with them. And if you say you will do something, they need to know they can count on your word. If you want your team members to be trustworthy, demonstrate trust.

Create an environment of support. Be a good listener, patient and open. Your team needs to feel they can express themselves freely. Trust builds trust.

Demonstrate that you value each team member's work. Every person has his or her own level of skill and responsibilities. Recognize that each one contributes to the success of the group.

Know your strengths and limitations. Evaluate and understand how you are perceived by the others. In particular, recognize your own weak points and work to eliminate them. Be able to speak about your failures with honesty and integrity.

Accept responsibility for your actions and those of your team. Demonstrate courage. If the team feels you are using them as a scapegoat, you will lose their respect and support.

Choose the Best Strategy

* ✳ *

When you watch *The Apprentice,* you get to see how the teams develop their strategies to fulfill the proposed tasks, as well as the disastrous effects of unsuccessful strategies. In one of the episodes from the first season, the objective was to manage a fleet of rickshaws and make as much money as possible after one day of work. The losing team's strategy concentrated on attracting more passengers. The winners, on the other hand, directed their efforts not only on attracting passengers, but also on selling advertising space on the vehicles. In other words, they proved to have more vision and developed a better strategy.

Developing a competitive and successful strategy requires a deep and complete understanding not only of your competitors, but of a series of other factors that can also influence your market position. It is just as important to know your organization's internal affairs as it is to know the external challenges and opportunities that exist on the outside. To develop a winning strategy, it is important to:

Know the market. It is essential to conduct research to determine which products are being offered to your target market and at what price. Without this basic information, you will be developing your products and price strategies in the dark.

Talk with your clients. Know your clients and their needs well. Know what they are saying about the competition. Expand your market by identifying the clients whose needs are not being satisfied by the competitors and develop products to meet these demands.

Identify the strengths and weaknesses of your organization. An honest evaluation of your company's resources, as well as the potential pitfalls, is fundamental for effective strategic planning. Optimize your strengths and weaknesses to take advantage of market opportunities. Be aware of your organization's weaknesses, especially those that can negatively impact your clients. To neglect that is to offer an advantage to your competitors.

Analyze your competitors' products. This analysis will give you ideas about how to improve your own offers and how to underscore the attributes of your products compared to those of your competitors.

Permanently monitor the competitions' plans. Become familiar with your competitors' marketing strategies. Understand the sales and service styles they employ so that you will be able to react against any move by the competition in a timely manner.

Create alliances that complement your strong points. Identify the partners that can fill in the existing gaps in your knowledge or potential. Remember: admitting to your weak points and knowing who to bring aboard to cover them is a sign of intelligence.

Regularly monitor your market. Your clients' needs and your competitions' potential can change frequently. An effective competitive strategy should change accordingly. Obtain new market perspectives through your clients and from others to validate your strategic plan and adjust it whenever necessary.

Anticipate the future. Understanding the competitive scenario is crucial to developing a winning strategy. However, to sustain a competitive advantage, it is equally important to define what the future will bring in terms of interests and needs. Without this connection between today and tomorrow, the chances for sustained success become minimal.

Know How to Form a Winning Team

* ** *

Those who watch *The Apprentice* know that few things irritate Donald Trump more than participants complaining about their own teams. One candidate who was severely criticizing his teammates heard the following: "Don't complain, solve the problem!"

Winning the respect and cooperation of colleagues and employees is fundamental to keeping the team cohesive and motivated. And without a cohesive and motivated team, there is no way to carry out any task successfully, because arguing, dissension, lack of motivation, and general discontent will always yield results short of what is desired. Therefore, do not forget to:

Take into account the group's mission before choosing your team. Choose people whose capacity and performance are the most appropriate to achieve the proposed objective. Do not make your choices based on personal relationships.

Organize a diversified team. Limiting the group to people with similar interests and experiences will limit the final result. Recruit individuals who represent different points of view and perceptions. If there is a need for support from different departments in the organization, include people from these departments in your team.

Know the strong points of each team member. Ask them which tasks they feel more prepared to perform in the project. This way, when you delegate tasks, you will know who is more prepared and more willing to take on the different roles.

Leave no doubt as to what you expect from each one. All members of the team need to clearly understand their responsibilities.

Do not lose focus. If you stay focused, the team members will clearly know the direction to follow. Always communicate your vision and involve everyone in discussions about what is being done, how it is being done, and why.

Do not create scapegoats. Analyze the entire team. If a single person is blamed for an eventual failure, it is a sign that the team was not in tune and it permitted someone to become overloaded or isolated. If victory belongs to all, then defeat cannot belong to one. In a cohesive team, poor performance by one team member is noticed and neutralized in time.

Keep motivated. Without motivation, even one's self-esteem is affected. Pay attention to signs of pessimism or low morale and do not allow the team's enthusiasm to wane. Publicly recognize each person's contributions, no matter how small, for that is a powerful motivational tool. On the other hand, authoritarianism, angry criticisms, and verbal abuse lessen everyone's good spirits, and they also indicate you are losing control and respect for yourself and for others.

Ask for suggestions to improve performance. New team members are generally able to see things the older members, out of force of habit, cannot notice. Even if you disagree with the suggestions presented, value the initiative of the person who made them.

Transmit Enthusiasm

* * *

Discouragement is contagious. In several episodes of *The Apprentice*, it was clear that whenever the leader of a team demonstrated indecisiveness, insecurity, and discouragement, the disheartenment spread like wildfire among the other group members. Leaders who are passionate about their opinions instill enthusiasm and motivation in their employees and colleagues, and they encourage them to achieve success. But the way you present your messages is fundamental to engaging others. Believe enthusiastically in your ideas. If you have conviction in your ideas, plans, projects, or direction to take, it will be reflected in your voice, in your words, and in your actions. Your passion will be apparent and will influence others. When communicating your ideas, do not forget to:

Build your case. Create a rational yet emotional foundation for your ideas. The intensity of your ideas, allied with facts and logic, will lead to the necessary support from your team.

Be direct and objective. Leaders who act in an assertive manner gain the respect of their collaborators because they express themselves in an honest and direct manner. When you speak in an assertive manner, you can express your point of view without disparaging or alienating the other team members.

Establish a dialogue. If you are always the only one to speak, you will end up speaking alone. Provide room and attention for other people's opinions, and they will feel motivated to participate.

Keep your cool. If your team members notice that difficulties make you lose your head or panic, pessimism will spread. Enthusiasm is not maintained with words, pep talks, and smiles alone. It is also of utmost importance to maintain a serene bearing when faced with difficulties.

Learn to Manage Conflicts

Not one episode of *The Apprentice* goes by without a fight or a misunderstanding among members of a team. That is not unusual, since conflict is a natural consequence of human interaction. Put two or more individuals together for a significant period of time and there will inevitably be a difference of opinion. When people face each other and disagree about a specific subject, they can become so obsessed in defending their points of view that they even stop communicating. That does not mean that misunderstandings cannot be productive: they can generate constructive dialogue through which new ideas can be generated and implemented. However, when conflicts prevent changes and destroy team spirit, it is necessary to know how to control them in time. And for that, you must:

Seek common objectives. Remind team members of everyone's mission. Stay away from personality-related issues. Ask them to reevaluate their goals and to concentrate only on common objectives. Once these objectives have been identified, the group can move on and discuss the means to share them.

Identify the focal point of conflict among team members. The more information you have about a misunderstanding, the better the chances you will have to solve it.

Gain the commitment of others. The objectives should be shared, but the means to reach them can vary. Reach a consensus to later move forward toward the achievement of common objectives.

Exercise professional courtesy. Rash demands only serve to alienate people. And what is worse, hostility can become infectious, affecting all team members.

Look beyond the problem. It may not necessarily be the situation that evokes anger but the perspective of those involved—which could lead to a serious conflict.

Find bases for an agreement. The team members may not have the same points of view, but they need a starting point to begin discussing a new idea. Have the team members recognize the differences of opinion and seek ways to eliminate the gaps or the divergences among them.

Confront problems in a confidential manner. If you need to confront a team member, do it in private. Shouting has no place in work. However, that does not mean you have to accept a mediocre performance or lack of cooperation from a team member.

Avoid hostility by reformulating conversation. Communicate with care. This is especially important when dealing with people with whom you have had some kind of misunderstanding. Advise them not to adopt a belligerent or sarcastic attitude.

Emphasize the positive aspects. When you notice the positive performance of colleagues who are hard to work with, immediately recognize their merit. Let them know their performance is being appreciated.

Maintain a pleasant environment. Speak in a frank, non-threatening manner. To speak in an open and honest manner with team members—especially those with whom you have had personality conflicts—can prevent future problems.

Be an Effective Project Manager

* ✳ *

Each episode of *The Apprentice* leaves no doubt as to the importance of the project manager; the one chosen to perform this function faces a true test. If he proves to be worthy of the responsibility and leads his team to victory, the project manager will have the unique opportunity to stand out from the rest and exhibit his potential. However, if he fails, he runs the risk of hearing Donald Trump direct his now famous sentence at him, "You're fired!"

An effective project manager is someone who finds solutions to execute complex and multifunctional tasks, within the given time and budget, but without the pretension of wanting to do everything himself. The ability to plan, coordinate, and execute projects requires, among other things, the capacity to lead and positively influence collaborators, guiding and motivating them to give their very best to reach a common objective. That's why, whenever you manage a project, remember to:

Clearly define the scope of the project from the very beginning. Transform the project's objectives and needs into concrete parameters for implementation. This is the best way to avoid having the project get out of control.

Define realistic deadlines to remain within the timeline. Execute this task together with all team members involved in the project. The key word is *realistic.* Your team will refuse to buy into the idea if it does not believe the deadline is feasible.

Break the project down into smaller and more manageable tasks. This will make the work less intimidating for team members, and it will help to conclude certain tasks within the established deadlines.

Delegate tasks based on team member competencies. Know the individual attributes of each team member and delegate tasks according to these attributes. Monitor the work to ensure the tasks are being performed as anticipated.

Estimate the impact that costs will have on the project. The manager must estimate all inherent costs for the project beforehand to be able to employ the available resources in a rational manner.

Show enthusiasm toward the project. A leader's enthusiasm inspires the others, helping to keep the team motivated and involved. Even if something does not work out as planned, demonstrate confidence to avoid discouraging the team. Positive attitudes will help the group overcome mishaps.

Instill and value team spirit. The members of your team should feel proud of being part of the group. If they are not enthused with past achievements and motivated concerning new objectives, their commitment will not be complete. This could create problems for you, making it more difficult to reach the team's objective.

Anticipate possible obstacles. Every project has its problems. Develop and give priority to contingency plans and know what the alternatives are to implement them when necessary. This will reduce the need for drastic measures and ensure the successful conclusion of your project.

Plan changes. During the execution of a project, changes may prove necessary. Always have an alternative ready that will help you to rapidly adjust the direction of your projects.

Keep a global vision. Instead of concentrating on the details of the tasks that should be executed, concentrate on the final objective. This way, you will be less vulnerable if a specific problem occurs along the way. Maintain a clear vision and prepare your project for the difficult moments.

Do not lose your project's "pulse." As leader, you have the obligation to monitor the progress of your team with regard to the tasks being carried out, as well as the application of resources. Do not reduce your participation. Your permanent involvement will help keep the project on track.

Delegate the Tasks Correctly

* ✳ *

Delegating tasks and responsibilities correctly is one of the biggest challenges faced by *The Apprentice* participants. Many times we see project managers succumb to the temptation of wanting to do everything by themselves or to take the opposite direction: delegate incumbencies without many criteria and lose control of the entire project. If the managers enter the board room and begin to blame the others for the failure, they will hear Donald Trump ask, "Why didn't you take control of the situation?" The apparently contradictory situation indicates the delicate equilibrium needed when it comes time to delegate tasks. On one hand, the leader needs to hear the opinions of the team and know when to accept them and when to reject them without causing any unease; on the other hand, it is fundamental for the manager to delegate responsibilities according to each individual's competence and ability. The idea here is not to choose the person who offers to execute a task, but the person truly capable of executing it. The person delegated to perform the task is responsible for its execution. However, the leader is always responsible for the final results. Therefore, do not forget to:

Establish objectives. Speak clearly to your team and explain the goals that must be reached for the project to be successful and determine what will be required to get there.

Make your team feel involved with the project. Motivate your collaborators to participate in developing the most appropriate strategy to reach the desired results. Be diplomatic but firm when accepting and rejecting suggestions. Although the final decision is up to the leader, it is important for the other members not to feel alienated from the process.

Choose the correct person for each task. When someone volunteers for a specific mission, be sure the person in question has the most appropriate background and skills to carry it out.

Provide directions. The person in charge of a task should have a certain degree of autonomy to execute it, but the leader provides the direction. Guide your collaborators without micromanaging.

Be sure everyone understands what you expect of them. It is impossible to delegate tasks successfully if the team members do not clearly understand what you expect them to do and the results they are to reach.

Avoid unpleasant surprises. Do not trust merely in what you expect members to do. Instead, be sure they are doing what is expected. Make constant follow-ups to accompany project development, but do it in a quick and objective manner. Do not permit these follow-ups to turn into endless, counterproductive meetings.

Know what to delegate and what not to delegate. Not everything can be delegated. Organizing the team, evaluating performances, and determining directions (and changes of direction) are exclusive responsibilities of the leader.

Praise and criticize. Praise those whose performances stand out and make a critical evaluation of those who underachieved. Do not allow others to play the "blame game." Each person must take responsibility for the task he or she took on, just as you will have to take responsibility for the final result.

Communicate Correctly With Your Boss

* * *

If there is anything that makes Donald Trump furious it is when a candidate tries to interrupt him repeatedly when he is speaking. *The Apprentice* audience has already witnessed this scene several times and must have been shocked by the total lack of tact demonstrated by some participants when addressing the boss. Knowing what to say and how to say something is fundamental. Therefore, always keep in mind the following hints:

Meetings demand preparation. Be careful with improvisation. Anticipate the questions that will be asked and be sure you are ready to answer them. Prepare all the material you must have beforehand. Forgetting a document or being ill prepared is an embarrassing sign of negligence.

Think before speaking. Do not expose yourself uselessly. In one episode of *The Apprentice*, one of the losing team members had immunity: that is, according to the show's rules he was not subject to possible dismissal because he had led the winning team in the previous episode. However, in his zeal to defend his performance, he said he had done such a good job that he was willing to forgo his immunity, because he was certain he would not be fired. The bravado ended up getting him fired.

Go straight to the point. Respond objectively to what you are asked. Do not exasperate your boss by beating around the bush with long-winded explanations and details that are not important.

Avoid biting your tongue and whispering. Say what you have to say in a polite yet firm manner. Using euphemisms, allusions, and indirect statements is not the same as being diplomatic. In reality, it seems as if you do not have the courage to defend your real opinion.

Seek the correct information. If your boss asks you a question and you do not have the information to answer it, the best way out is to be honest and say you need more information before answering. Guessing, beating around the bush, or giving incorrect data will only make matters worse.

Timing is everything. Especially if you have to discuss a raise, a promotion, or a personal issue. It is a sure path to disaster to try to talk about this with bosses when they are busy dealing with an urgent company problem or when they are feeling the impact of some bad news or mishap. Use your sensitivity and good sense to notice if it is the appropriate time or not.

Know how to argue. Do not confuse argumentation with arguing. If you need to go against the will of your boss, be sure you use solid argumentation. Have hard data such as numbers, data, and facts; and not merely opinions. Keep a cordial tone and avoid shouting matches and confrontations. Do not face the situation as a dispute. Bosses have the final word, but you can help them reach the most appropriate decision if you supply useful information.

Pay attention to body language. When speaking with your boss, stay alert and attentive. If during the conversation your boss notices you seem bored or uninterested, your image will suffer.

Learn to Launch and Position a New Product

* ✳ *

Many of the tasks in *The Apprentice* involve launching or positioning a new product in the market. To be successful in this task, on the show as well as in real life, you must first know the market for which the new product is targeted. This knowledge is very important when it comes time to elaborate the launching strategy, but it is far from the only ingredient for success. Intangible factors such as intuition and feelings also play a fundamental role in this process. Therefore, always consider the following factors:

Believe in the product. Before convincing the buyer, the product must convince the seller.

Establish marketing objectives. Clearly define the goals that should be reached for the product to be a success.

Know the consumer public. There is no way to create a winning marketing strategy without knowing exactly at whom the marketing should be aimed. Know the target audience's habits, likes, preferences, and expectations.

Study the competition. You must know who you will compete against. Research similar existing products on the market and analyze their strong and weak points. This will show you the advantages of your product and what makes it better or different from the others. These are the aspects that will guide the entire marketing campaign.

Find out how to stand out. In an extremely competitive market, it is not sufficient for your product to be the best. Everyone must *know* your product is the best. A lousy marketing strategy will bury even the most brilliant ideas.

Set the right price. How much should your product be sold for to make a profit? What is the expected profit? Does this fit the socioeconomic profile of your target market? The answers to these questions are crucial to determining the feasibility of the new product and avoiding losses.

Know How to Behave in a Job Interview

* ✳ *

At the end of the first season of *The Apprentice* there were only four candidates left. They had all stood out in performing the tasks proposed by the show, and the time had now come for them to go through a series of interviews conducted by members of the Trump Organization. Two candidates were eliminated based on their performances during the interviews, and two remained to participate in the final test. In other words, even in a reality show that relied on tasks in which the participants demonstrated their skills, interviews played a decisive role in the final phase. Therefore, when you need to go through a job interview, remember to:

Study the employer. You will certainly hear questions about the company's products or what type of contribution you could make if you got the job or why you would like to work there. The only way to avoid vague and generic answers is to have information about the company beforehand.

Emphasize your strong points and be prepared to talk about your weak points. Of course, your main interest during an interview is to highlight your qualities. However, questions about your weak points will surely come. Think before hand about the best way possible to answer them.

Expect the unexpected. Interviewers may not limit themselves to asking questions. They may invite you to participate in some group dynamic, ask you to take a written test, or ask you to evaluate some aspect of the company. Consider these possibilities so you do not get caught off guard.

Better to be formal than too informal. Some interviewers try to give a more relaxed tone to the interview to break the ice. But that does not mean you can act as if you were at home, talking with friends. Being formal does not mean to behave in a rigid, tense manner, but to behave according to the occasion and to watch both verbal and nonverbal signals. No matter how friendly the interviewer may seem, remember that you are being observed the entire time.

Remain alert. Listen carefully to the questions and be objective with your answers.

Demonstrate confidence. Self-confidence is a quality that the interviewers always look for in prospective employees. Not even the most brilliant resume will help a candidate who projects an insecure and hesitant image.

The School of Life:
The Entrepreneur's Classroom

* ✳ *

At the end of the first season of *The Apprentice*, the decision was between two candidates: one of them, Kwame, had a brilliant academic background. The other, Bill, mainly stood out for his boldness in dealing with practical matters. Both had done very well during the competition. However, Bill defeated Kwambe and was declared the winner. Why did that happen?

A professor in the graduate program at FAAP in São Paulo, César Adames, dealt with the question in an article about the show published in *Qualimetria* magazine. According to Adames:

> Whereas Kwame comes from a traditional school that gives priority to knowledge acquired from books, courses, and training, Bill graduated from the corporate world's school, where he lived the kinds of successes and failures every entrepreneur is subject to, even having gone to a good university. The lesson that remains from *The Apprentice* is that the job market is always interested in that something more each candidate can offer individually.[11]

What would that "something more" be? Intuition, a sense of opportunity, motivating enthusiasm, equilibrium, vision, the desire to learn, in short, everything that characterizes the gen-

---

[11] *Revista Qualimetria*, no. 161.

uine entrepreneurial spirit and that transforms someone into a true master in the art of selling an idea in three minutes.

Many of the sixteen candidates for the program had diplomas and titles obtained from some of the most prestigious academic institutions in the world. Although such resumes carried their weight when the sixteen candidates were chosen from among hundreds of thousands of people trying to participate in the show, in the end, that was not what made the difference. The winner was the one who demonstrated the smarts, the skills, and the leadership qualities necessary not only to do well in the tasks proposed by the reality show, but also in the real-life management position in one of the Trump Organization companies.

I do not disdain in any manner or form the value of academic education, but I question the excessive importance given to diplomas and titles. It is possible to achieve success in business by allying knowledge acquired in college with entrepreneurial capacity. However, the opposite is impossible. No one becomes a successful businessman if he has a vast academic resume but does not demonstrate any entrepreneur spirit. Normally, people like that need to align themselves with business geniuses in order to prosper. Brilliant minds need a good entrepreneur to sell their ideas. No matter how fantastic their creations, they would run the serious risk of starving because they would not know how to sell them.

I attended two colleges and I dropped out of both, because the businesses I was involved in at the time consumed all my time and energy. I cannot say I have any regrets. I have always found ways to learn and acquire knowledge; after all, those who do not stay current with the times are quickly surpassed. However, I never gave up on the implementation of an idea or abandoned a business just getting under way. If I did, how could I have ever learned what only experience can teach?

Early in life I realized that true entrepreneurship is only learned by being an entrepreneur. That is, you must take risks and act. While still a child, I used to sell comic books at the door of the building where I lived. At the age of sixteen, I was responsible for the sound equipment at my friends' parties, and I would reinvest the money I made in new equipment and records. At that time, I did not let one business opportunity slip past me. My friends used to spend their vacations in the United States and bring back videogames and videocassettes that had not been converted. I immediately began to represent a company that did the converting and made a commission every time a friend became a client. These early demonstrations of initiative were my training program. They were my 3Rs in entrepreneur school. Having ideas and seeking opportunities and the means to transform them into businesses became as natural as breathing. Thus, a few years later, when I read that article about Elite models in *Photo Magazine* I visualized an opportunity and went about achieving it.

The fact is we are all apprentices in a reality show called *life*. The situations caught by the cameras on *The Apprentice* are no different from the ones we face every day: the need to overcome obstacles; to sell an idea in three minutes; to stand out in the middle of a crowd; to deal with people of the most varied personalities, attitudes, behaviors, and mentalities; to seek cooperation even in the most adverse environments; to remain righteous and motivated despite opposition from the "King Sadims" of the world, to learn from our errors and come out on top; to believe when no one else believes; and so on. The award can be a $250,000-a-year job or the job you have always wanted, a promotion, professional recognition, a doctor's office full of patients, a finalized deal, a closed sale, a prosperous business, or the implementation of a project that benefits the needy. After all, you are the one to define the measure of your success.

Chapter 8

LEARNING
From The MASTERS

*"Some men see things as they are and say why
—I dream things that never were and say 'why not'?"*
—George Bernard Shaw

Now that you understand the theoretical part that involves selling an idea in three minutes, it is time to see how it works in practice. The stories in this chapter are of people who were successful because they knew how to transform their dreams into reality. Driven by a profound inner conviction, they followed their intuition, overcame obstacles, and gave life to their ideas in the form of successful businesses or social initiatives that are improving the society in which we live.

Everyone highlighted in these stories possesses the characteristics that define an entrepreneur. These are:

They are guided by their vision. Entrepreneurs do not see things as they are, but as they could or should be. This vision is so powerful that they never lose sight of it, and never rest until they are able to transform it into reality.

They have a sense of opportunity. Aware of everything that directly or indirectly has to do with their vision, entrepreneurs are always discovering, evaluating, and exploring opportunities. They frequently create opportunities where none seemed to exist.

They ally intuition with experience. Through a process that is partly unconscious and partly conscious, entrepreneurs combine intuition and experience to evaluate the potential of their ideas, anticipate possible obstacles, and outline their strategy.

They are achievers. Entrepreneurs are driven by an imperious need to build and achieve. The creative spirit leads entrepreneurs to look for new niches to be explored and new opportunities for growth. At times, they will even leave behind a successful business and go in search of new ideas.

They are motivators. The enthusiasm, conviction, and strength with which entrepreneurs believe in their visions are contagious and capable of motivating partners, investors, collaborators, employees, and even complete strangers.

They are persistent. For entrepreneurs, obstacles are challenges, and failures are seen as motivation for them to learn from their mistakes and try again. If a person gives up after the first, second, or third difficulty, it is because their entrepreneurial spirit has yet to be awakened.

They are negotiators. Do not confuse an entrepreneur's persistence with blind stubbornness. Entrepreneurs fight for their ideas, but also know how to give in when necessary to achieve a greater objective. Their elevated social intelligence makes them masters at negotiations.

They are pioneers. The fact that something has yet to be done does not discourage the entrepreneur. Quite the contrary, it is a stimulus to try what has yet to be tried. The entrepreneur is an innovator par excellence.

They generate prosperity. Entrepreneurial action generates economic progress not only for the entrepreneur but also for society. In the case of the social entrepreneur, actions generate direct benefits and an improvement in the quality of life for the less-favored members of the population.

The following pages detail lessons from those leaders who specialized in transforming ideas into reality.

Amador Aguiar

———— ✳ ✳ ✳ ————

FOUNDER,
BRADESCO

Amador Aguiar, an extremely poor peasant, ran away from home at the age of sixteen. He never finished elementary school and even got to the point of sleeping on park benches. However, despite all these adversities, he was already showing signs of the character that would transform him into a true winner. Once, when a restaurant owner offered him a plate of food, the young Aguiar replied, "No, first I want to work, and then I'll accept your food." And he really did work, at many different jobs, until in 1926, at the age of 22, he became an office boy at the Birigui (SP) branch of the NoroesteBank.

Aguiar knew how to make something out of nothing better than anyone else. At night, he had difficulty sleeping because of his asthma. But he was able to transform that problem into an instrument for success. He would spend his nights reading everything he could get his hands on about banking activities, and he soon outdid many other employees who had college degrees. In just two years, he was a bank manager.

In 1943, he was hired as managing director of the Casa Bancária Almeida (Almeida Bank), in Marília (SP), and he received 10 percent of the shares of what would become the

Banco Brasileiro de Descontos, or Bradesco. Under Aguiar's command, Bradesco revolutionized the financial system. The financial experts of the time had an elitist view of business, and they were only interested in doing business, with farmers and big industrialists. Bradesco changed this mentality by becoming the first Brazilian bank to invest in retail. Managers who used to remain hidden in their offices were now sent out to the front of the agencies. Never forgetting his humble origin, Aguiar instructed his employees never to return a check that was filled out incorrectly: they were to call the clients over and politely show them how to use their checkbooks. "Never lend much to a few, but a little to many," was one of his favorite sayings. Always on the lookout for opportunities, Bradesco was the first bank in the country to accept electronic bill payments, the first to receive income tax returns, and the first to use computers on a large scale. And that is how it became the largest private bank in Latin America. On the front of Bradesco headquarters in Osasco (SP), it is still possible to read a saying that always inspired Aguiar, "Only work can produce wealth."

SOURCE: Ricardo Bellino, *Stone Soup: Ten Ingredients for How to Create Your Recipe for Success,* Rio de Janeiro: Campus/Elsevier, 2003.

Rolim Adolfo Amaro

* ✻ *

FORMER PRESIDENT,
TAM AIRLINES

The man who left his mark on the history of Brazilian aviation had a modest childhood in the interior of the state of São Paulo, where he lived with his family in a thatched-roof house without electricity or a bathroom. At the age of 13, Rolim Adolfo Amaro had to drop out of school to begin work, doing a little of everything: a trucker's assistant, a woodcutter, and even carrying logs in a sawmill. But, at the age of 17, he decided the time had come to realize his big dream: to get his pilot's license. He had to work several odd jobs at the Catanduva Air Club to pay for the course, and he had to sell everything he had to pay for the final exam. With his license in his hand, Rolim went to Londrina and tried to get a job in an air taxi company. He got the job, but without pay. The sacrifice was worth it in order to remain near his beloved planes: he used to clean the aircraft, eat leftovers from passenger meals, and sleep in the hangar, using newspapers as his blanket. His efforts yielded results. After some time, Rolim was hired as a pilot for Marília Air Taxi (TAM). However, since he was the last pilot on the schedule, he would only have the chance to move up the list if the client handpicked him. That was when he learned a lesson about the importance of winning the client that would change his entire life.

An invitation to fly in the Araguaia made him leave his job and transfer to the region with his family. They lived in a brick house with a roof made of palm tree leaves, but the sacrifice was not in vain. Rolim was able to buy his first airplane and just two years later, he boasted a fleet of 15 aircraft. And his rise did not stop there. Rolim was invited to become a partner at TAM and assume management of the company. His innovative initiatives and his strategic vision turned TAM into one of the most successful companies in the country. When he died in a helicopter accident in 2001, TAM had reached the mark of thirteen million passengers transported. When drawing up the company's conduct norms, Rolim included a rule that expresses his true business spirit very well, "When in search of excellence, good is not sufficient."

SOURCE: http://www.tam.com.br

Edson de Godoy Bueno

———— ✳ ✳ ✳ ————

FOUNDER,
AMIL

It was possible to detect a talent for business at a very young age in Edson de Godoy Bueno. Born into a poor family, he became a shoeshine boy at the age of 10 and he created a new service concept: in order to beat out the competition, he began to tend to his clients at their homes. School was never his strong point, and so it was quite a surprise when the boy decided to study medicine. But he strived so hard he was able to achieve his dream.

In Rio de Janeiro, where he studied medicine, he was chosen to work as an on-duty doctor at the São José Clinic, in the Baixada Fluminense district. The clinic was practically bankrupt and did not pay its employees. After working for six months without getting paid, Bueno proposed that he be made a partner in the clinic using the salary they owed him as his capital.

After a few years, São José became the largest maternity hospital in the entire state. The hospital's recovery generated enough cash to acquire yet another hospital, which generated enough cash to acquire another, and then another . . . and the chain kept expanding until Amil was founded in 1978.

Bueno had to get out of medicine to dedicate himself full-time to manage his business, and the Amil success story is the best example of his talent as a businessman. In 2003, the company earned $2.5 billion. But his conquests do not stop there. In the book, *Beyond Maxi Marketing,* published in 1994, authors Stan Rapp and Thomas L. Collins tell the stories of some of the most successful companies in the world. Amil was included in this select group. Even in times of rampant inflation, the company was able to grow at a rate of 45 percent per year for 10 years running, earning $800 million in a country whose economy is a mere tenth of the size of the American economy.

Perhaps the basic ingredient for Bueno's recipe for success can be summed up by a single word: *passion.* As he once stated in an interview, "You have to feel passion for what you do. That feeling is a determining factor for success."

SOURCE: Ricardo Bellino, *Stone Soup: Ten Ingredients for How to Create Your Recipe for Success,* Rio de Janeiro: Campus/Elsevier, 2003.

John Casablancas

* ✳ *

FOUNDER AND FORMER PRESIDENT
OF THE ELITE MODELS GROUP

John Casablancas became a legend in the glamorous world of fashion. Founder of Elite, which in its golden days was the largest modeling agency in the world, he allied his business talent with a keen aesthetic sense to discover and introduce to fame some of the greatest models of all time—Cindy Crawford, Naomi Campbell, Linda Evangelista, and Gisele Bündchen are just some of the names on his list. He was the number-one model agent in the world for 20 years. Then, he decided to sell his part of the business and due to the contract he signed, he had to stay away from the modeling business for five years. But that period of time has already passed, and now John Casablancas is back in grand style. His new mission is to discover the new supermodels for the 21st Century. And there is no one better than Casablancas for the job. After all, his last great discovery was Gisele Bündchen and no one has yet to introduce another star like her. To achieve this objective, John Casablancas is getting ready to launch Starmodel in partnership with Rede TV!

A true revolution in the world of traditional contests, Starmodel intends to discover the new star for international fashion, and she will receive an award never before granted in a contest of this kind: $1 million in work contracts with Elite in New York. Besides the model category, Starmodel will also look for new stars in the categories of actress, TV hostess, fashion stylist, and musical talent. Starmodel is the first chapter in John Casablancas' megaproject called Starsystem, the largest international platform for launching and promoting courses, seminars, and contests geared toward all those who are trying to get started in the world of modeling, cinema, TV, fashion production, and other media activities. The project also foresees the creation of the largest international network of modeling and talent agencies, StarNetwork. Starsystem also marks the return of my commercial partnership with Casablancas, which began in 1998, when I brought Elite to Brazil. After showing the project to the co-owning partner at Rede TV!, an agreement was immediately reached. It was one more idea sold in three minutes.

SOURCE: Ricardo Bellino, *POI—The Power of Ideas: How to Transform Ideas into Strokes of Success*. Rio de Janeiro: Elsevier, 2003.

Carrie Chiang

* ✳ *

THE CONDO QUEEN OF MANHATTAN

Carrie Chiang is a Chinese woman who lived for 15 years in Brazil. At the age of 45, after her divorce, she decided to restart her life in New York. But in order to keep her family's lifestyle, Carrie realized she would have to find a suitable job, even though she had never worked before. While searching for something to do, she took the realtor's course with Barbara Corcoran, president of the Corcoran Group. In a short time, Carrie became the greatest broker in Manhattan, breaking all sales records. Today she is the vice president of the Corcoran Group and her annual sales pass the U.S. $100 million mark. With a client list that includes names such as Robert DeNiro, Barbra Streisand, and Donald Trump, Carry is known as the "Condo queen of Manhattan." And there is a good reason for this. In the 1980s, when the New York real estate market faced a tough crisis, she sold, at one time, no fewer than 90 flats in Trump Palace. So what is her secret? Her son Stanley Chiang answers, "My mother is frank, honest, and direct. She always speaks the truth and the clients known they can trust her completely."

SOURCE: Ricardo Bellino, *Midas and Sadim*
(Rio de Janeiro: Campus/Elsevier, 2005).

Victor Civita

———— ✳ ✳ ✳ ————

FOUNDER,
ABRIL PUBLISHING GROUP

Daring was definitely not lacking in an Italian living in the United States by the name of Victor Civita, when in the mid-1940s, his brother César showed him a very risky project. César lived in Argentina, where he had founded a publishing house that had been named Abril. He had just obtained the rights to produce and market the Donald Duck comic book in South America from Disney. César was very unsatisfied with the political situation in Argentina and he proposed that his brother be in charge of installing the Abril publishing house in Brazil. Unlike César, Victor had never worked in publishing. But that did not prevent him from immediately accepting this job and moving to São Paulo. That is where it all began, in a little room on Libero Badaró Street.

The idea seemed to have everything going against it. Victor couldn't speak Portuguese, and he did not know the local market. His choice of São Paulo to start activities was also highly criticized because the city was considered a province that did not have the necessary journalists, graphic artists, and resources to create a successful publishing house. But, a man ahead of his time, Victor believed in the potential of the business and of the city as well. On July 12, 1950, the first Donald Duck comic book was released. In a short time, the publishing house was inaugurating its first print shop. And it never stopped growing. Victor never let the smallest detail slip by unnoticed. He would visit Antonio Prado Square, where the newsstand owners would gather to get the sections of the newspapers in the wee hours of the morning, and he would talk with them and ask them to display the Donald Duck comics in prominent positions on their stands. In the 1960s, he noticed an opportunity linked to the development of the automobile industry and he released *Quatro Rodas* magazine. And, aware of the demands of the growing middle class, he decided to forgo cultural division—against the opinion of his directors, who claimed the product was too sophisticated for the Brazilian public.

And so, the publishing house that Victor founded in Brazil became the Abril Group, one of the largest communication conglomerates in Latin America, which publishes 150 titles and reaches thirty million readers. Its graphic park prints approximately 350 million magazines per year. When he died in 1990, Victor left the group's companies to his two sons. But he made a point of leaving the money he had in bank accounts, stock, and personal property to the foundation that bears his name and which he created with the objective of promoting education.

SOURCE: http://www.abril.com.br

Laércio Cosentino

* ✳ *

FOUNDER AND PRESIDENT
MICROSIGA SOFTWARE

At the age of twenty-three, Laércio Cosentino was a young engineer who worked as an intern in a company called Siga, which specialized in developing programs for mainframes, when he had an ingenious idea: why not develop the same programs for PCs? This story is another example of the power of ideas. Thanks to his initiative, even though without any capital, Laércio ended up forming a partnership with his boss, Ernesto Habekorn. Siga was renamed and became Microsiga. It faced its true test when it debuted in a market that besides being highly competitive is also subject to unfair competition from piracy. But the challenges were overcome successfully. Today, Microsiga is the leader in the software market for small and mid-sized companies. With two thousand employees and 60 offices, it has annual earnings of $190 million. Part of Cosentino's success is based on a fundamental principle: recognizing the value of employees.

Besides paying good salaries, the businessman makes a point of maintaining personal contact with his team. "The success of a company is the success of a group," he says. Thanks to this philosophy, technology professionals actively try to work at

Microsiga, which permits the company to keep some of the best talent on the market.

When speaking of the lessons he has learned in his trajectory as an entrepreneur, Cosentino says, "The most common mistake an entrepreneur commits is to not give up control of an aspect of the business when he/she does not have the competence to handle it. Strategists and visionaries are not always the best in day-to-day operations. It may be one of the most difficult things to do, but you must be able to recognize your own weaknesses."

SOURCE: http://www.Professorcezar.adm.br/Textos/Cinco LicoesdeEmpreendorismo; http://www.empreen dedordoano.com.br/2003/2_2_2000_hall.php

Amilcare Dallevo, Jr.

* ✳ *

PRESIDENT OF
REDE TV!

At the age of fourteen, and having lost his father, Amilcare Dallevo, Jr., found himself in a situation where he had to work to support his family. His first job was something that no longer exists today, a computer card perforator. Years later, he received a degree in electrical engineering and began to work in bank automation at Itaú. He did so well that in a year and a half, he was hired by Citibank to take care of telecommunication management. But, at the age of twenty-seven, he left all of that to work in a tiny room, which was the headquarters of his first company, Tecnet. His biggest trump card was in developing a pioneer system that permitted the issuance of telephone bills per extension, making it easier to manage telephone bills at companies. In just two years, his client list included such companies as Embratel, Ultra Group, Itaú Bank, and Citibank, where he had begun his career. His modest room soon became a five-story building.

Dallevo's biggest stroke of genius was the creation of a system through which the public could interact with television programs in real time over the 900 line. The system started in 1993, when for the very first time, the audience could watch the Rio de Janeiro samba school parade and vote on their favorites during the presentations. The success was so great that Dallevo opened another company, Tecplan, and he began to supply his technology to several television networks. Globo Network, for example, used it for the audience to cast their votes in the now extinct *You Decide,* a ratings leader at the time. With the capital he accumulated with these initiatives, Dallevo took his next step and bought five TV Manchete concessions together with his partner, Marcelo Carvalho de Fragali.

And that is how Rede TV! emerged, making Davello and Fragali the newest members of the select team of great businessmen in Brazilian television.

Source: http://terra.com.br/istoegente/01/reportagens/dallevo.htm

Michael Dell

* ✳ *

In 1984, a nineteen-year-old decided to bet everything on an innovative new idea: the creation of a company that would sell computer products and services directly to consumers, eliminating the middleman. In this case, "everything" totaled the $1,000 he was able to gather along with all his effort and creativity. In just fifteen years, that sun has multiplied many times over. His company, Dell Computers, became one of the largest personal computer companies in the world, with 33,000 employees in thirty-four countries. According to *The Wall Street Journal,* Dell is the number-one company in terms of financial return for its investors, and has been named by *Fortune* magazine as the most admired company by Americans. Today, the company created by a kid who believed in his idea, occupies 56th place in *Fortune's* ranking of the 500 largest companies. And if that were not enough, it is the only company on the list whose revenues have had an annual growth of more than 40 percent for three consecutive years.

With the objective of promoting entrepreneurship, Michael Dell founded EO (Entrepreneurs' Organization), a nonprofit organization whose mission is to educate and encourage entrepreneurs from around the world through a mutual support network (see more information in Chapter 10). The entrepreneurial spirit that guides his actions is summarized by Dell in a single sentence. "There is always an opportunity to make a difference."

SOURCE: http//www.askmen.com/men/january00/8c_michael_dell.html; http://www.dell.com

Antonio Ermírio de Moraes

———— * ✳ * ————

CHAIRMAN OF THE BOARD
OF THE VOTORANTIM GROUP

Antonio Ermírio de Moraes represents the third generation of the family at the helm of the company founded by his grandfather, the Portuguese immigrant Antonio Pereira Inácio, and then expanded by his father, Senator José Ermírio de Moraes. Votorantim is among the largest conglomerates in Brazil, and it is comprised of companies that are leaders or hold a prominent position in areas ranging from the production of cement, steel, and paper to chemical products and orange juice. It is also a presence in the financial, biotechnology, and information technology sectors. However, for Antonio Ermírio, success was not simply handed over to him. In 1945, when he went to study engineering in the United States, the heir lived for four years in a room at a boarding house eating sandwiches to economize. Upon returning to Brazil, he was warned by his father that the work that awaited him at the family businesses was only a test. "If things don't work out, I'm not going to hire you," said José Emírio. But he proved to be up to the challenge. In six years, he founded his own company, the Companhia Brasileira de Alumínio (Brazilian Aluminum Company). In 1962, Antonio Ermírio assumed control of all of the companies and Votorantim did not stop growing, inaugurating cement, zinc, and nickel factories. The group, which employs 25,000 workers, reported $27 billion in assets in 2002.

In his more than 50 years at Votorantim, Antonio Ermírio almost never took a vacation, and he begins work religiously at seven o'clock in the morning. Discrete, disciplined, not accustomed to the life of luxury so common to people in his position, Antonio Ermírio likes to say, "The day you see me driving a Ferrari, you can put me in a straightjacket and send me to a mental institution, because it will mean I've gone crazy. In a country such as ours, you cannot drive around in a car like that for status. Status has to come from intelligence."

SOURCE: http://www.terra.com.br/biblioteca/brasileiro/empreen dedor/emp5.htm; www.votorantim.com

Marco Aurélio Garib

———— ✳ ✳ ✳ ————

FOUNDER,
EVERSYSTEMS GROUP

In the beginning of the 1990s, the popularity of ATMs and magnetic cards did not go unnoticed by an entrepreneur in search of a good opportunity. An electronics engineer, Marco Aurélio Garib believed that the market was promising and he was willing to take risks. He left a secure job and founded, EverSystems, which would end up revolutionizing the home banking sector, making it possible to carry out financial transactions over the computer. One of the company's first missions was to develop and implement a home banking system for Unibanco in 1991. The success was immediate. In just three months, the system had won over 10,000 clients. In 1993, EverSystems began to offer wireless solutions for sending secure financial information by pager. Six years later, Garib innovated once again—now at a global level—by creating e-mail banking. And more innovations are on the way, such as the development of a mobile payment system, which permits making payments from your mobile phone.

In 14 years, Garib's entrepreneur vision elevated EverSystems to an enviable position. Today, the company serves 80 percent of the Latin American home banking market, with an installed base of more than 2.5 million users. Also noteworthy is the fact that before Citibank signed an Internet banking contract with Garib for its Latin American branches, the U.S. National Security Agency and the FBI made a sweep of the system created by the Brazilian engineer to test its security and reliability. Garib's system passed with flying colors and the contract was signed.

SOURCE: http://inventabrasilnet.t5.com.br/eversys.htm;
http://empreendedosdoano.com.br

José Alencar Gomes da Silva

——— ✳ ✳ ✳ ———

FOUNDER OF
COTEMINAS AND VICE PRESIDENT OF
BRAZIL IN THE LULA ADMINISTRATION

Born into a modest family, José Alencar was one of 15 children in the Silva family. By the time he was seven, he was already working behind the counter of his father's store in the village of Itamuri, in Muriaé township, in the state of Minas Gerais. When he was 14, he felt it was time to go in search of new perspectives, and he went to work in a store in Muriaé. The salary was so low he couldn't even rent a room, so, he would sleep on a cot in the hallway of a hotel. He moved to Caratinga, which is also in Minas Gerais, and he continued working in commerce until the age of 18, when his older brother lent him money to open his own business, a fabric store. José Alencar did not spare any effort to make his company prosper. In order to economize, he began to sleep behind the store's shelves on a bed improvised out of crates and a straw mattress. He decided he was going to take the minimum amount of profit possible for his personal expenses, and reinvested the rest in his store. A skillful negotiator, he used to say, "To negotiate never hurt anyone, so haggle as much as you can." Later, he sold his store and received the capital to found what would become Coteminas—Companhia de Tecidos do Norte de Minas (Northern Minas Textile Company).

José Alencar became a senator and vice president of the Republic. His son, Josué Christiano Gomes da Silva, an entrepreneur just like his father, took over the position of finance director at Coteminas in 1992, at the age of 29. At that time, the company had three factories, produced 8,000 tons of fabric, and its annual earnings were $60 million.

Today, Coteminas has 11 factories, produces 110 thousand tons of fabric, has annual earnings of around $1 billion, and it owns the Artex, Calfat, Santista, Garcia, Attitude, and Jamm brands.

SOURCE: Francisco Britto and Luiz Wever. *Empreendedores Brasileiras* (Vols. 1 and 2). Rio de Janeiro: Elsevier, 2003/2004.

Wayne Huizenga

* ✳ *

FOUNDER OF
WASTE MANAGEMENT, BLOCKBUSTER,
AND AUTONATION

This North American descendant of a Dutch family is a phenomenon of world entrepreneurism. Huizenga is the only person in history to have more than six companies listed on the New York Stock Exchange and the only one to have three companies enter the Fortune 500: Waste Management, world leader in garbage collection and management; Blockbuster, a giant in the video rental sector; and AutoNation, the largest automobile retailer in the United States. Huizenga was born in Chicago and moved to Florida in his teens. After a few odd jobs, he began to work for a garbage collection company. With a great deal of persistence, he was eventually able to convince the owner to sell him part of the business. He was not afraid of hard work. Huizenga would drive a garbage truck from two o'clock in the morning until mid-day, and then in the afternoon he would visit clients.

The story goes that at that time an acquaintance from his schooldays saw him behind the wheel of a garbage truck and felt sorry for the "ungrateful fate" of his former school classmate. Little did he know that he had seen the very beginning of Waste Management, a multimillion dollar company that became one of the biggest garbage collection and management companies in the world. But a great entrepreneur is not only the person who creates a successful business out of nothing: sometimes his intuition helps him see that the potential of a certain company is being underused. So he buys the company and takes it to unimaginable heights. That is what happened with Blockbuster, which in 1987 was a $7 million business with 19 stores. Soon after Huizenga and two partners took over the business, the video rental chain became an enterprise worth $4 billion and had more than 3,700 stores spread over 11 countries.

In 1994, when Blockbuster was sold to Viacom, it was worth $8.4 billion on the NYSE. Huizenga's next step was to found AutoNation, the first national automobile retail chain in the USA. This is just a brief summary of his businesses, which also include incursions in the sports area—Huizenga is the current owner of the Miami Dolphins of the National Football League. For these triumphs, he was honored in 2005 with the prestigious Ernst & Young World Entrepreneur of the Year.

SOURCE: http://www/eu/cp,/global/content.nsf; International/ World Entrepreneur_Of_The_Year_Awards_2005_ Winner_Of_WEOY_2005; http://entrepreneurs. about.com/od/famousentrepreneurs/p/wayne huizenga.htm

Jorge Gerdau Johannpeter

—————— ✶ ❈ ✶ ——————

PRESIDENT OF
THE GERDAU GROUP

It was not without reason that Jorge Gerdau Johannpeter was given the nickname "man of steel." He owns 16 steel mills that earn $2.27 billion per year and he produces 6.6 million tons of steel in Brazil and four other countries. This story began at the start of the 20th century, when a family of German descent opened a nail factory in Porto Alegre. The business was doing well until of World War II when it became difficult to find the raw material necessary for manufacturing nails. That was when Curt Johannpeter, Jorge's father, made a very daring move: instead of trying to find the scarce raw material, he would manufacture it. And so, he sold family properties and gathered the necessary money to buy the Riograndense Steel Mill. His son Jorge started at the bottom—and at a very early age. At the age of 14, he was already working in the factory, operating the machines to produce nails. Later, he studied accounting at night while he worked in the company office during the day. In the 1960s, alongside his father, he coordinated the company's growth as they acquired several other companies and factories and spread across state borders, and later national borders. Jorge progressively went through every area in the group until becoming president in 1983. Today, the

Gerdau Group is ranked 35th in the world in steel. "I am a competitive being and a fanatic concerning quality," says Jorge.

This search for quality is not only manifested in the way he conducts business, but also in his initiatives in social entrepreneurship. He leads the RS Quality Association, which has the objective of improving the efficiency of public and private institutions in the state of Rio Grande do Sul. In one of its actions, the association was able to reduce the waiting time at the Santa Casa de Misericórdia Hospital in Porto Alegre from eight hours to only thirteen minutes.

SOURCE: http://www.terra.com.br/istoe/biblioteca/brasileiro/
empreendedor/emp11.htm

Kirk Kerkorian

———— * ✳ * ————

Deal Maker and
Former CEO of MGM

The name of billionaire Kirk Kerkorian is always followed by the title, "father of the megahotel/casinos" in Las Vegas. It was a long journey for the descendant of Armenians, who at the age of nine was selling newspapers to help his family. During his teen years, his occupations included everything from boxer to Air Force pilot. His contact with aviation inspired him to start his first business. In the 1940s, he bought a plane with the money he had saved as a pilot. His first client was a merchant who would rent the plane to fly from Los Angeles to Las Vegas, and the capital of gambling left a deep impression on Kerkorian. Later, when the company grew into a charter flight business, Kerkorian grew the company's capital and with the dividends he accumulated, he decided to invest in Las Vegas. His first initiatives involved buying and sell-ing land in the city. After some time, he had enough capital to build his first hotel-casino based on an idea no one else had believed in at the time, which was to transform the Las Vegas hotels into gigantic resorts for family vacations. Many people told him it would never work. But Kerkorian did not give up. "You have to ask a ton of questions and listen to people. But, in the end, you have to let your own instincts guide you," the billionaire would comment later. At the same time he was investing in Las Vegas, Kerkorian began to turn his attention toward the movie industry. Under his control, the MGM studios underwent restructuring, mergers, sales and resales, becoming a conglomerate with ramifications in the hotel business as well. At the time of its inauguration in 1973, the MGM Grand Las Vegas was the largest hotel in the world. Seven years later, the hotel caught fire, but Kerkorian did not waste any time: in a mere eight months he rebuilt and reopened the MGM Grand. In 1986, he sold the MGM hotels for a half billion dollars. The current MGM Grand, which opened in 1993, has 5,000 rooms and a theme park as big as Disneyland was when it opened in the 1950s.

SOURCE: http://www.1st100.com/part3/kerkorian.html; http://www.armeniapedia.org/index.php?title=kirk_ kerkorian.

Samuel Klein

* ✳ *

Samuel Klein has probably heard people tell him his life story would make a good movie many times. That is the first thought that comes to mind when anyone hears the incredible story of this Jewish immigrant who escaped certain death in a Nazi concentration camp to become the king of retail in Brazil. Klein was born in Zaklikov, Poland. He learned to be a carpenter from his father. When the German army invaded his country during the Second World War, he was taken with his father to Maidanek, the third largest Nazi concentration camp. His mother and his younger brothers and sisters were taken to Treblinka, where they died. In 1944, when the Russian army arrived in Poland to free them from the Germans, Klein and the other prisoners were sent off to Auschwitz, the most feared of all concentration camps. Since there were no more trains, they would need to travel the 50 kilometers on foot. When they stopped in a vast wheat field, Klein found the perfect moment to escape.

Despite the risk, this was probably his only chance at survival. He asked one of the soldiers to excuse him for a minute while he relieved himself and then ventured into the wheat fields. Very carefully, he began to make his way through the field. The next day he was terrified when he heard dogs barking. But he was greatly relieved when he met up with some Polish Christians who were also hiding from the Germans. The Poles gave him food and helped him escape.

Klein was able to make his way back to his old house, which had been completely destroyed. He went to work in a small nearby farm in exchange for food. At the end of the war, he reencountered some of his brothers and sisters and went to Germany, where to his great surprise, he found out his father was still alive. Samuel wanted to immigrate to the United States, but that was not possible because the quota had already been filled. He was able to get a visa to Bolivia, but at the time, the country was on the brink of a revolution. And that is how Samuel, already married and with a small child, had to immigrate once again, this time to Brazil.

He settled in São Caetano do Sul, in Greater São Paulo, where he began his fascinating career as a merchant. He bought a horse and buggy and became a street peddler, selling bed, table, and bath linens door to door. After five years of hard work, he had already gathered enough money to open his first store, which in time would multiply in an amazing manner. Today, Casas Bahia has more than 300 stores spread around the country. The chain is bigger than the sum of its five main competitors.

When speaking about his success, Samuel Klein says, "One plus one equals two. But, one idea plus one idea is equal to thousands of ideas."

SOURCE: Ricardo Bellino, *Stone Soup: Ten Ingredients for How to Create Your Recipe for Success* (Rio de Janeiro: Campus/Elsevier, 2003).

Henrique Meyerfreund

* ✳ *

FOUNDER
GAROTO CHOCOLATE

At the end of the First World War Henrique Meyerfreund, a 23-year-old German, and founder of the Garoto Chocolate factory, left Germany, which had been devastated by the war, and immigrated to Brazil. Without any money and living as a guest at a friend's house in Vitória, in the State of Espírito Santo, Meyerfreund began to make cinnamon candies to sell on the Villa Velha square. He soon built a little shed behind the house, hired more people, and began to increase production. Business kept growing and it soon became a company, H. Meyerfreund, founded in 1929.

After his father's death, he used the money he received as an inheritance to buy chocolate machines used in German factories, and with those machines, he began to produce chocolate in Brazil. However, regardless of the name he had made selling candies, he faced great difficulties in selling chocolate because at the time, a company called Lacta dominated the market, without any competition. But the German immigrant overcame all the obstacles and expanded his company, which began to be called Garoto, in honor of his first clients, the young boys who used to buy his cinnamon candies. In the 1940s, during the Second World War,

Meyerfreund had already become such a dear and respected person in Vitória that the residents of the city protected his factory from destruction in reprisal for Germany's actions in the war.

Meyerfreund stayed at the head of Garoto from 1929 to 1971. His philosophy was to always produce good quality products at an affordable price. When he died in 1972, he left his heirs the most modern chocolate factory in Latin America. When his son, Helmut, became president that same year, Garoto was manufacturing 5,000 tons of chocolate per year. When Helmut left his position as president, between 1999 and 2000, the company had a productive capacity of 135,000 tons per year.

The company that was born from the candies a German immigrant used to make in his friend's kitchen was recently sold to the largest food company in the world, Nestlé, in a deal involving millions of dollars.

SOURCE: Ricardo Bellino, *Stone Soup: Ten Ingredients for How to Create Your Recipe for Success* (Rio de Janeiro: Campus/Elsevier, 2003).

Lírio Parisotto

———— * ✳ * ————

FOUNDER AND PRESIDENT,
VIDEOLAR GROUP

In 1988, a company by the name of Videolar revolutionized the market for manufacturing videocassette tapes (VHS). Behind this success stood Lírio Parisotto, former owner of a modest video rental store, who at the helm of Videolar had his dream recognized when he received the "Entrepreneur of the Year for 2002" award in the Master of Business category—the largest entrepreneurship event in the world. Everything began in the 1970s, when Parisotto traveled to New York and saw, for the first time, a videocassette player. In awe of the possibility of watching selected movies at home, as well as being able to record and re-record images without any need for developing the film, he wasted no time to cash in on the opportunity.

Back in Caxias do Sul, a client of Parisotto ran into financial difficulties and offered to sell Parisotto his company using the debt as part of the payment. Parisotto agreed and that was how he opened the first video club in the state. The club also sold sound systems and electronic products. Having graduated in medicine, Parisotto gave up on the idea of any practice and decided to dedicate himself to his new business. In 1985, during a trip to Tokyo at Sony's invitation, he saw the laboratory used for subtitling and recording videocassette tapes. At that exact moment, his intuition told him he was seeing a unique opportunity. Something that particularly caught his attention was the fact that the tapes were wound at perfect lengths for subsequent recording. In other words, they had the exact amount of tape for the duration of the movie, without any waste, contrary to what was being done in Brazil at the time.

Upon returning to Brazil, he sold his electronics store and began to produce the new tapes. In a short time, he launched an unprecedented product on the market: tailor-made pre-recorded tapes for distributors and other clients. In 1990, Parisotto transferred his factory to São Paulo and opened another in Manaus. The company quickly expanded its area of operation, which today ranges from the manufacturing of polystyrene (the basic raw material for his products), to the delivery of recorded media (videocassette tapes, DVDs, and CDs) right to the client's doorstep. "The foundation of Videolar has something in common with the history of other entrepreneurs, especially in a country like Brazil, in the respect that there are abundant opportunities to set up a business beginning with a good idea, profession, or market niche. Besides that, the rest is 10 percent inspiration and 90 percent perspiration," says Parisotto.

SOURCE: http://www.videolar.com.br

Sílvio Santos

* ✳ *

Sílvio Santos was the absolute best at making something out of nothing. At the age of 14, Señor Abravanel, the son of a simple family of immigrants that lived in Rio de Janeiro, decided it was time to start earning some money. His first step was to observe how the street vendors operated downtown. He studied their sales tactics, where they bought their merchandise, and what they did. He soon noticed something that would help him throughout his lifetime: the secret was to know how to attract an audience.

In a matter of days, the adolescent who was just starting out was already selling much more than all the other veteran street vendors.

At the age of 18, Sílvio Santos was working as a radio announcer, but he felt he could make much more money in commerce. And ideas were something he had in abundance.

Since he had to use the Rio-Niteroi ferryboat every day, he soon had the idea to install a system of loudspeakers so the passengers could listen to music, and of course, Sílvio could broadcast ads between one song and the next. The idea quickly expanded, and he was soon selling beverages on the ferryboat. His work as a radio announcer took him to São Paulo, and there he found another business opportunity. A friend told him he had bought into the idea of selling people a Christmas basket containing surprise presents, which the client would pay for in installments over the year. It just so happens that the partner who had sold him the idea was not able to administer it. The people were not receiving what they had bought and the business had turned into a giant headache.

Many people may think that only a fool would get into such a business. But Sílvio was able to see what others could not. He took over the business, which operated out of a basement, paid off its debts, made contracts with toy and household appliance manufacturers, and began to sell tens of thousands of baskets. . . . And that is how Baú da Felicidade was born.

Meanwhile, he traveled with a type of circus caravan and received the nickname of Talking Turkey. The reason for the nickname was because the man who would become the greatest communicator in Brazil was so shy that he would turn beet red whenever he had to talk in public, no doubt another stone with which he made more soup.

His activities as a businessman, announcer, and caravan show master of ceremonies, as well as his fantastic ability in dealing with the public, ended up converging in television. In 1961, he appeared for the first time in an evening program on TV Paulista, present-day TV Globo. And the rest is history. Today, the founder and owner of SBT (Sistema Brasileiro de Televisão) is not only a wealthy businessman, but he is also synonymous with success.

SOURCE: Ricardo Bellino, *Stone Soup: Ten Ingredients for How to Create Your Recipe for Success* (Rio de Janeiro: Campus/Elsevier, 2003).

Luiz Seabra

—— * ✳ * ——

FOUNDER OF
NATURA

In the middle of a conversation with his sister, Luiz Seabra had an intuition that would change his life. At the age of 12, Seabra heard his sister say that her dream was to be an esthetician to dedicate herself to taking care of people's skin. "She was speaking, and I had this thought, like it was coming out of my heart, an intuition. So I said, 'I'm going to produce the products those people will use,'" remembers Seabra. But a long time would go by before he would be able to make that childhood dream become reality.

Seabra had to start working at the age of 15, yet he still managed to graduate in economics and began to work in the razorblade division of a multinational company. Since he had no experience in the subject, he began to read everything he could about skin, so that he would be able to suggest improvements for the products. However, the razorblade division ended up closing its doors and Seabra, who was not feeling very satisfied at the company, decided he was not going to stay. That was when life placed an opportunity at his feet that would lead him to the fulfillment of his childhood dream. After being casually introduced to the owner of a small cosmetics laboratory, Seabra was invited to manage the enterprise. He accepted, but that was not enough to keep him happy. One of the things that bothered him was the stereotyped view that beauty and cosmetics had at the time. He wanted to develop a line of products that would appeal to the self-esteem of people, and not just be seen as ordinary "makeup;" he wanted something that would contribute to a new awareness of the relationship between mind and body. A partnership with Jean Pierre Berjeaut, the son of the owner of the laboratory in which Seabra worked, led to the foundation of Jeberjeaut Indústria e Comércio de Cosméticos Ltda., which four months later, would change its name to Natura. The newly established laboratory operated out of a warehouse, and its entire capital was equal to the value of a VW Beetle. During the first five years, the difficulties were so great that even his partner thought seriously about giving it all up; however Seabra never lost his enthusiasm.

Natura survived recessions, economic crises, inflation, partnership reform, and much more. By the year 2000 the company had 3,100 employees and approximately 300,000 consultants (saleswomen) spread all over the country, becoming the largest national cosmetic company, standing out for its pioneering spirit with regard to social actions and environmental preservation.

SOURCE: Francisco Britto and Luiz Wever. *Empreendedores Brasileiros* (Vols. 1 and 2). Rio de Janeiro: Elsevier, 2003/2004.

Viviane Senna

* ✳ *

MENTOR AND PRESIDENT, AYRTON SENNA INSTITUTE

Two tragedies marked the life of Viviane Senna da Silva Lalli. The first was the death of her brother, Ayrton Senna; a formula 1 driver and idol, in 1994. A short time later, Viviane lost her husband in a motorcycle accident. The misfortunes, coupled with her wealth, could very well have led her to a more reclusive and quiet life. However, Viviane opted for a different path. A little before his death, Senna had told her about his desire to help the needy children of Brazil. Viviane decided to transform his dream into reality. That was how the Ayrton Senna Institute was born on March 21, 1995, with the objective of using the Senna and Senninha brands and the pilot's image to raise funds for social projects.

Viviane had a degree in psychology, but she had never worked in managing the family's businesses. She has proved to be a top-notch social entrepreneur. "I do not give donations, I make social investments," she says. She does not receive any salary for her work at the head of the institute. "My profit is to see that the quality of life will improve for these children," she says and then adds, "Our programs have clear goals for the future. We want to change this country." Today the Ayrton Senna Institute assists in managing and supplies financial support to 24 social projects geared toward the education of forty thousand children in 10 different Brazilian states.

SOURCE: http://premioclaudia.abril.com.br/1997/sena.html;
http://senna.globo.com

Donald Trump

———— * ✳ * ————

Chairman and President of
the Trump Organization

Determination, boldness, and *daring* are words that always come to mind when the topic is Donald Trump. A real estate businessman whose buildings became landmarks on the New York skyline, Trump has already faced a few setbacks—the worst of them in the beginning of the 1990s, when he had an accumulated debt of $9.2 billion, but he was able to negotiate with the banks and come back out on top. His personal fortune is estimated at $5 billion and his reality show, *The Apprentice,* is among the most watched programs on television. And it is Trump himself who tells the beginning of his success in his testimonial in my book *POI—The Power of Ideas* (Rio de Janeiro: Elsevier, 2003).

"I wanted to be successful, but I wanted to do it my way. My father had been successful in real estate, but I wanted to triumph on my own. Since I always appreciated beauty in construction, it was my logical choice. The first business I undertook was to buy a bankrupt hotel. No one was willing to give me any support, much less credit, but the project ended up being a great success. Although it had gone bankrupt, the Commodore Hotel was well located next to Grand Central Station. The hotel was truly in terrible shape. Actually, that whole area was pretty well abandoned at that time. There was potential, but the risk was also high. Well, to make a long story short, I wanted a really fantastic building, so I looked for an architect with wonderful talent, Der Scutt, who soon became as excited as I was with the idea of the new hotel. The Grand Hyatt Hotel you see today next to Grand Central Station reflects the station itself, the Chrysler Building, and all the other reference points that may go unnoticed without it. Almost every critic and preservationist who hated the original conception defends it with enthusiasm today. There were times when I faced various obstacles and setbacks, but I am a very obstinate guy. You have to be that way to be successful and to overcome obstacles and adversity. I saw that as a passing situation and ensured myself it would be but a tiny hitch in a grand journey."

SOURCE: Ricardo Bellino, *POI—The Power of Ideas: How to Transform Ideas into Strokes of Success*. Rio de Janeiro: Elsevier, 2003.

Sam Walton

✳ ✳ ✳

FOUNDER OF
WAL-MART

Sam Walton is a classic example of a man with vision. Although he had a college education, it was the school of life that truly taught him. Walton was born and raised in an impoverished rural community in Missouri, during the Great Depression. After the war, Walton and his wife, Helen, got a franchise for a Ben Franklin store in the city of Newport, Arkansas. Thanks to the couple's efforts, the store, which operated in the red, became one of the most profitable in the state. However, jealous of the couple's success, the owner of the store asked for it back, and Walton and his wife had to move to another city and start over again. The couple and Walton's brother, James, opened a small variety store in Bentonville, also in Arkansas. Ten years later, they had 16 branches.

A man before his time, Walton applied such innovative concepts as the generous use of discounts and self-service. It demonstrated in practice that the entrepreneur sees things no one else sees. Walton was tired of hearing others say that self-service would never work, because people were accustomed to being waited on by clerks. But history proved Walton right. The Bentonville store gave rise to Wal-Mart, a company that reached the year 2000 with annual earnings of over $100 billion and also gained the title of being the largest single employer in the United States. Another successful initiative by Wal-Mart is its partnership with philanthropic institutions to benefit local communities. When listing the golden rules of successful people, Walton wrote, "Swim upstream. Go the other way. Ignore conventional wisdom. . . . I think that in all these years, what I heard the most was: 'a city with less than 50 thousand inhabitants cannot maintain a discount store for a long period of time.'"

Time proved Walton right.

SOURCE: Peter Krass. *The Book of Business Wisdom.* Rio de Janeiro: Campus/Elsevier, 1997.

Chapter 9

TESTING
YOUR SKILLS

* ✴ *

"Few are open to conviction,
but the majority of men
are open to persuasion."
—Johann Wolfgang von Goethe

After everything that has been said about intuition, strategy, social intelligence, and entrepreneurship, it is time to stop and reflect: how does all this apply to you? Or, how do you apply all of this to your life?

The tests that follow will give you valuable clues to help you evaluate these questions. You can answer them in the book and then transfer the answers to the online versions of the tests that you will find on the site www.youhavethreeminutes.com. If you prefer, you can answer them directly at the site. The results will be sent to the e-mail you provide.

Test 1:
Discover Your Entrepreneur Quotient
(E.Q.)

* ✳ *

Objective: Measure the E.Q., or Entrepreneur Quotient, the degree of skill you have for being successful in the business world. Each correctly answered question in this first test is worth 10 points. Therefore, whoever answers all 18 questions correctly will have an E.Q. of 180, which means a very high degree of skill to be successful.

1. In a job interview, the most important thing is to:
    a. Answer all questions in a brilliant manner.
    b. Have excellent credentials.
    c. Project responsibility and confidence to the interviewer.

2. If your boss rejects one of your ideas, you should:
    a. Rethink your idea, or even rethink your job.
    b. Always insist. After all, you believe in the idea.
    c. Stop talking about ideas to your boss so that you don't become annoying.

3. The person who thinks big . . .
    a. Has more chances to achieve great results.
    b. Takes too many risks, and should therefore learn to control himself or herself.
    c. Is going to definitely get into trouble.

4. When asking for a raise, the most important thing to do is:
    a. Clearly explain the reasons you deserve the raise.
    b. Choose the right moment to talk to your boss.
    c. Demonstrate to your boss that you feel undervalued.

5. When you notice that a business you truly believe in is taking a long time to work out, your attitude is to:
    a. Forget about it and move on.
    b. Blame your collaborators.
    c. Be persistent.

6. To be passionate about what you do is:
    a. Out of the question.
    b. Essential for success.
    c. Something that could wear you down and consume your energy.

7. In order to build a good reputation, it is necessary to:
    a. Fulfill what was promised.
    b. Invest in advertising.
    c. Be seen with influential people.

8. To trust one's own instincts is:
    a. Risky.
    b. Doubtful.
    c. Necessary.

9. Complete the sentence: "We should be optimistic, but . . ."
    a. keep our feet on the ground.

    b. it's not always possible.

    c. nothing else. We should be optimistic, period.

10. Complete the sentence: "A leader has the right to be defeated, but he doesn't have the right to be . . . "

    a. Fair.

    b. Moderate.

    c. Surprised.

11. What are the essential requirements for someone who wants to work with a businessman like Donald Trump?

    a. Be sure people feel comfortable in your presence, have a sharp mind, be creative, loyal, and trustworthy.

    b. Be smart, a hard worker, a good talker, and daring.

    c. Have a perfect résumé and seek perfection in everything.

12. In the business world, your personal principles should be . . .

    a. Maintained only when convenient.

    b. Always maintained.

    c. Forgotten.

13. For a businessman, patience is:

    a. Fundamental.

    b. An obstacle. It is necessary to always act quickly.

    c. Something the others should have, but not you.

14. An essential characteristic for a negotiator is:

    a. Inflexibility.

    b. Arrogance.

    c. Flexibility.

15. When we negotiate with someone, we should:
    a. Be aware of the other person's needs.
    b. Only be aware of our own needs.
    c. Be aware to make the most profit possible.

16. To close a deal is a matter of . . .
    a. Persuasion.
    b. Power.
    c. Insistence.

17. To get out of a crisis, you should:
    a. Hire more lawyers and assistants.
    b. Retake control of the situation.
    c. Have a brilliant idea.

18. The best way to get a return when you invest is by:
    a. Taking risks.
    b. Using good sense.
    c. Betting on novelties.

Test 2:
Do You Ally Intuition With Strategy?

* ✳ *

Objective: Find out how actions and decisions are influenced by intuition, rational thinking, or a combination of both.

1. When you meet someone for the first time, you:
   a. Trust mainly in what your intuition says about the person.
   b. Trust more in the references others gave you about the person.
   c. Listen to your intuition, but also evaluate information from other sources.

2. If your intuition tells you something will not work, you:
   a. Give up immediately.
   b. Try to better evaluate the situation, but with caution.
   c. Believe in the evidence, even if it contradicts your intuition.

3. When you close a deal, you:
   a. Base your actions on facts, but you also consider your impressions and feelings about the transaction and the people involved.
   b. Base your actions only on facts.
   c. Base your actions only on impressions and feelings.

4. Your strategy is based on:
   a. Intuition, available information, and previous experiences.
   b. Available information and previous experiences.
   c. Only on intuition.

5. When you have little time to analyze a great deal of information, you:
   a. Use your intuition to select what to analyze.

b. Try to get more time.

c. Feel difficulty working in such situations.

6. When you have an intuition about a new business, you:
    a. Are immediately convinced it will work.
    b. Believe it may work, but go about evaluating its feasibility.
    c. Doubt it will work and give up so you don't waste your time.

7. When you put an idea into practice, you:
    a. Follow your plan rigidly.
    b. Only follow your intuition and do not stick to any plan.
    c. Use your intuition to provide more flexibility to your plan.

8. Which of the three sets of characteristics below best describes you?
    a. Intuitive—pragmatic—self-confident
    b. Organized—rational—perfectionist
    c. Intuitive—restless—impulsive

9. If your intuition contradicts consensus, you:
    a. Begin to doubt yourself.
    b. Begin to doubt the consensus.
    c. Ignore it and follow the consensus.

10. To you, intuition is:
    a. An important tool.
    b. Your only compass.
    c. Something you do not trust.

Test 3:
Are You Midas or Sadim?

* ✳ *

Objective: Find out if you have a Midas touch or if your characteristics make you more like King Sadim.

1. When comments arise about someone's slip up, you:
   a. Listen with interest.
   b. Try not to get involved.
   c. Want to know all the details.

2. When you obtain embarrassing information about the personal life of someone you don't like, your reaction is to:
   a. Spread the information, but take care so as to not compromise yourself.
   b. Save the information to use it at the right time.
   c. Ignore it.

3. In a conversation, gossip and malicious comments are:
   a. A waste of time.
   b. Added seasoning.
   c. The main point of interest.

4. Everyone is talking about the latest scandal involving a well-known person. You:
   a. Try to get informed to not be left out.
   b. Try to not get informed if it has nothing to do with you.
   c. Try to see what advantages you could gain from it.

5. When someone is in trouble, you:
   a. Act like you have always acted toward the person.
   b. Comment on the problem, but never in front of the person involved.
   c. Your reaction will depend on what is most convenient for you at the time.

6. If you dislike someone, you normally:
   a. Try to forget about the person if you cannot resolve your differences.
   b. Do not rest until you get your revenge.
   c. Strive to unmask the person in front of others.

7. When a person asks you to keep something a secret, you:
   a. Spread the news. If the person truly wanted to keep it a secret, he or she would not have told you in the first place.
   b. Only tell your friends.
   c. Keep the secret.

8. If in a conversation gossip arises about a successful person, you:
   a. Get interested. After all, it is good to know we all have our weak points.
   b. Try to hide your interest to demonstrate your superiority.
   c. Suspect what you have heard. After all, success attracts envy.

9. When you hear someone speak badly about another, you:
   a. Try to change the subject.

b. Feel it is your duty to tell everything to the person who is the target of the comments to warn him or her.

c. It depends. If you think the person in question deserves it, you will add your negative comments to the conversation.

10. If you are obliged to put up with an incompetent partner or boss, you:

a. Disclose as much as you can about the other person's faults to show you have nothing to do with all this.

b. Allow the other person to expose him or herself.

c. Try to pull the rug out from under the other person to speed up his or her fall.

Test 4:
Discover Your Degree of Initiative

* ❋ *

Objective: Check if you have sufficient initiative to make your business or career take off.

1. My motivation to begin a new enterprise stems from:

a. Myself.

b. Positive reactions from others.

c. Knowing someone has done this before and it worked.

2. How do I relate with people?
    a. I prefer a small, but trustworthy, circle of friends.
    b. The degree of intimacy may vary, but I always try to expand my circle of relationships.
    c. I don't waste my time with people I have nothing in common with.

3. My team follows me . . .
    a. Because I am the boss.
    b. Because they believe in me.
    c. Because I don't give them any other alternative.

4. Responsibility is . . .
    a. A burden I must carry.
    b. Something we assume in order to grow.
    c. A trap: to be responsible for something is the same as becoming a scapegoat.

5. At work, when the opportunity arises to volunteer for something, I . . .
    a. Let it go. I already have too much work.
    b. Accept. It could be the opportunity I was waiting for.
    c. I try to send some other fool in my place.

6. Hard work is something that . . .
    a. I only do to achieve an immediate objective.
    b. I do because the others are never able to handle it.
    c. I do because it is my main capital investment.

7. If I need to make a quick decision . . .
    a. I use my intuition and don't waste time.

b. I give someone else the responsibility. That way I avoid getting burned.

c. I refuse to do it. I don't work well under pressure.

8. When people disagree with me . . .
   a. I try to see who is right.
   b. I maintain my position at any price.
   c. I pretend to accept and then do what I want.

9. If my effort doesn't seem to be taking me anywhere, I . . .
   a. Double my effort.
   b. Reevaluate my effort and my objectives.
   c. Give up. It's a sign that it wasn't supposed to work out.

10. If I feel I have already done everything there is to do in my job, I . . .
    a. Stay on just for the salary.
    b. Stop trying. If they want to they can fire me.
    c. Seek new motivations—or a new job, if necessary.

Test 5:
Do You Know How to
Leave A Good Impression?

* ✳ *

Objective: Evaluate the impression you leave on others and the degree of awareness you have about this.

1. When I meet someone for the first time I . . .
   a. Always have the feeling that I talk too much.
   b. Feel uneasy and speak as little as possible.
   c. Try to talk naturally.

2. In a conversation in a social environment, the important thing is to:
   a. Make my point of view very clear.
   b. Establish a pleasant exchange of ideas.
   c. Demonstrate what I know and beat around the bush with what I don't.

3. In a first meeting, I try to speak about myself . . .
   a. Whenever possible. After all, the other person doesn't know me.
   b. Little by little, according to the interest demonstrated by the other person.
   c. I hate to talk about myself.

4. To speak about my own property and status is . . .
   a. Inappropriate. It could look like I was forcing myself on the other.
   b. An excellent way to make the other person know who he or she is talking to.
   c. I am proud of what I have. If someone thinks I am forcing myself on them, then that's their problem.

5. To speak about work with someone I have just met is . . .
   a. An excellent idea, because I could talk about that for hours.

b. Something that should be done with care to not tire the other.

c. A good opportunity to expose my collection of office jokes.

6. When I talk with someone whose likes and opinions do not coincide with me, I:
   a. Try to find points in common.
   b. End up arguing.
   c. Stop talking.

7. To do well in a conversation, one must:
   a. Talk well about many things.
   b. Talk well about many things, but also know how to listen.
   c. Know many funny stories.

8. When you get dressed for a first meeting, you:
   a. Choose the appropriate clothes for the occasion.
   b. Wear the most expensive clothes in your wardrobe.
   c. Don't worry about it. The important thing is what people are on the inside.

9. During a party, you are introduced to someone who could help you in your business. You:
   a. Feel very embarrassed.
   b. Go straight to the point and don't miss out on the chance to ask for something.
   c. Start a pleasant conversation, and if it is not the right time to talk business, try to set an appointment for a future meeting.

10. When people start to talk about themselves, you:
    a. Start thinking what you could say about yourself.
    b. Pay attention and give signs of empathy.
    c. Find it all very boring and try to take control of the conversation.

Chapter 10

CONCLUSION

Throughout this book we have discussed the factors that will allow you to succeed in selling your idea in three minutes. Now, the time has come to talk about what happens after your idea is sold. You could say this is the moment the real work kicks in. You earned the opportunity you wanted so badly and now you must show you are worthy of the trust that has been confided in you. But, just like everything else in life, this does not have a straight path, but rather a circular movement. The finish line, when you close the deal, the contract, or the promotion, is also a new starting line. Your performance when you fulfill what you promised will allow you to form valuable capital, the only kind that truly matters: the necessary credibility to consolidate your successes and seek new initiatives.

However, fulfilling what you promised and solidifying your credibility does not represent the end of the line. At most, they are landmarks that signal the conclusion of one stage and the beginning of another. Once again citing John H. Johnson, the man who built a publishing empire out of nothing, "You always have to face the task of starting over and prove to a new audience just how good you are."[13] And thank goodness that is how things are. Of what use would so much effort, sweat, and sacrifice be if we became prisoners of a single conquest, of a single success? Of what use would it be to reach an objective only to become stagnant in the glories of the past, to become some fossil that no longer learns, progresses, and evolves?

Part of this evolutionary path frequently consists of knowing when to pass the baton, knowing when to delegate functions and allow your idea to grow wings of its own and conquer the world. The same happens when we raise our children: there is a time when they need help and protection. Then, as they develop, it is necessary to allow them to walk on their own two feet, make their own decisions, in short, experience for themselves the transformation process of going from child to adult. Things are no different in the business world.

After my idea of implementing the Elite branch in Brazil became a success, and after this success established itself, I realized it was time to move on. The same thing happened with the Fashion Targets Breast Cancer campaign, and it is with great joy that I see the seed I planted continue to give so much fruit so many years after moving aside to seek new objectives. And finally, the time came to pass the baton, or the golf club, for Villa Trump. My mission as a man of ideas was completed: I had transformed my intuition into a project, and the project into an enterprise that has every reason to become a landmark in the world of real estate. I was able to sell the idea to Donald Trump and gather the ideal investors for the enterprise to take off, and

---

[13] Cited in Peter Krass (1997).

then I reached a decisive moment in which ego, or vanity-driven attitudes could have ruined everything. Once the enterprise had a solid foundation, its development required the presence of a specialist with proven experience in real estate development. It needed someone capable of dealing with all the necessary technical aspects for us to move on to the next phase, which was the construction itself. Since I am not an engineer, nor do I have any experience in any area related to engineering, I handed over control of Villa Trump to Victor Foroni, founder of Método Engenharia and the most qualified person to take over the helm of the enterprise at this new phase. As founder and deal maker for Trump Realty Brazil, I continue as shareholder and member of the board through my holding company, Haret Participações, but the golf club, so to speak, is now in Foroni's hands.

And so I now have the time and resources to follow my new dream: to promote and stimulate entrepreneurship through the Instituto do Empreendedor (Entrepreneur Institute), the acronym of which in Portuguese is Inemp (www.inemp.org), an institution whose basic premise is to foment entrepreneurial activity. One of Inemp's first initiatives is the Empreenda Network, an educational and communicational platform comprised of a magazine, a radio program, a television show, a series of books called The Entrepreneur's Library, and a partnership with Ernst & Young to promote the world-famous World Entrepreneur of the Year award. This award, which is the largest world event of its kind, will have its national and Latin American chapter coordinated and organized by Inemp starting in 2006.

My intent is to transform Inemp into a worldwide initiative, starting with a branch in the United States, which will work to promote the exchange of ideas and business opportunities between entrepreneurs in both countries.

Inemp is also promoting an international campaign to preserve the endangered rainforests. U.S. poster artist Milton Glaser (creator of the logo "I Love NY") is designing its logo. Brazilian composer Almeida Prado is writing its theme song, and pianist João Carlos Martins will perform it.

Inemp will be one of the platforms of my new business venture, Bellino's Unlimited, an idea bank that is conceived based on the proposal of fomenting and enabling the implementation of ideas so they may become successful commercial enterprises.

Awakening the Entrepreneurial Spirit, Inemp is an initiative that will represent a landmark in Brazilian entrepreneurism. Much has been said about the need to invest in education, to stimulate entrepreneurism, and to assist in shaping our new businessmen. Except for some honorable exceptions, little has been done about it. In reality, there are very few legitimate or noteworthy initiatives. The importance of stimulating and developing the Brazilian entrepreneurial spirit is undeniable. No nation can grow without the entrepreneurial strength of its people. Without it, we run the risk of succumbing to the "sleeping giant" syndrome, "lying eternally on its splendid land" (a parody of the Brazilian national anthem) and always waiting for the time to rise, which never comes, or the change that never occurs, for the miracle; in short, everything that is the antithesis of the entrepreneurial spirit. Therefore, Inemp will:

- Promote and spread the entrepreneurial initiative at all levels of society, stimulating the creation of new entities and promoting socioeconomic development.

- Serve as a source of information for entrepreneurs' opinions, attitudes, expectations, management styles, and administration techniques.

- Facilitate the sharing of ideas among entrepreneurs.

- Promote the entrepreneurial initiative through participation in several public and private programs that stimulate, recognize, and foment the entrepreneur.

- Work together with other institutions interested in promoting the entrepreneurial initiative.

- Act as a defender of the entrepreneurial initiative, including support for legislation that is favorable to business in small to mid-sized markets, as well as partnering with economic development organizations to help them fund new businesses and develop national projects to support the entrepreneurial initiative.

- Participate in the creation, organization, and spreading of events whose objectives are to identify, foment, and reward entrepreneurial initiatives, especially through the Empreenda Summit.

Another of Inemp's concerns is social action. My main source of inspiration is the work of an old friend, Sami Goldstein, whose story is worth noting. After a long and successful corporate career, spending more than thirty years at IBM where he reached the position of vice president and finance director, and after a 10-year adventure in retail as a partner in Fotóptica at the traditional

Óticas Fluminense in Rio, Sami now wants to help his peers. After volunteering in several Jewish associations and relief entities, he began to see, among his colleagues, friends, and relatives clear signs of the impoverishing of the middle class. Ever more frequent stories about the cancellation of health insurance plans, the transfer of children from private back to public schools, the selling of assets for cash, the selling of club memberships, and late payments of loans indicated to him that something needed to be done.

The enormous pool of recently graduated young adults combined with the dismissals generated by the avalanche of mergers and the need for companies to cut costs resulted in the shaping of a middle class figure he calls the *new poor*. These are professionals who graduated more than 15 years ago, had good salaries, but who did not keep pace with the innovative technologies that emerged and then simply lost their jobs. Society knows how, or at least tries, to take care of the conventional poor. Foundations, NGOs, Zero Hunger, food stamps, unemployment insurance, hospitals and public schools, churches and many other associations, and institutions take care of them. But who takes care of the new poor?

According to Sami, they need temporary help to get out of the situation in which they now find themselves. They are backed into a corner, depressed, disoriented, and many try to cover up the difficulties they are going through, do not ask for help, and feel embarrassed when they do. Rather than examining the sad side of the story, Sami saw an opportunity to join the forces of those on top to help these people get back on their feet with dignity. Instead of assistance programs, he created a true support network in which professionals and companies do not donate money, but time and work. The goal is to produce a solidarity network that can provide answers for a new social need, recruiting and organizing volunteers who would initially operate along two fronts. "We begin with health and employment, but we want to go much further," says Sami.

The starting point was health. Sami and his team of volunteers divided the city into regions. Then, they made a survey of doctors' offices for several specialties, laboratories, and clinics in each region. The next step was to visit these doctors, laboratories, and clinics. With very few exceptions, they all agreed to donate a certain number of patient visits. To convince them to collaborate, Sami underscored the importance of engaging in social action as a volunteer, and he also reminded them that those being benefited were people who found themselves in temporarary financial difficulties but that once they got of this situation they could become paying customers.

All of the information about the donated services was gathered at the volunteers' central office. Now, they needed to contact the new poor who needed medical assistance.

Several institutions, such as schools, clubs, religious centers, and many other possible locations where the new poor could be found were visited by volunteers who were trained to conduct interviews and detect needs. Those people who were identified by the volunteers were referred to the central office, which would then be responsible for making the appointments.

Meetings were held every month with the volunteers and the professionals to evaluate the progress of the program. Since the beginning of the project three years ago, more than 2,600 families have been treated.

But Sami was still not satisfied. There was more to do. The next step consisted of helping the new poor return to the labor market. It was up to the volunteers to make a registry of companies that normally hired middle-class employees with college education and to develop a professional placement program for this type of labor. The program includes partnerships with schools, which offer English, computer, business courses, and others, as well as resume writing, preparation for interviews, and reestablishing the candidates' priorities and perspectives.

The resources to begin the project, promote it, and set up the central office were obtained through private donations and an international organization. Fund-raising is done every year in order to maintain the program.

This lesson teaches us that the entrepreneurial spirit can and should be applied to corporate initiatives, but also to social actions, which is why it gets the name of social entrepreneurship. Many times, everyday pressures place us in a kind of glass room in which only our interests and personal needs fit. The result is that this individualism ends up allowing, perhaps even more than other factors, for social ills to proliferate and intensify. And so, we blame the government, the interest rates, the dollar, the crisis, the War in Iraq, or any other war of the moment, and everything remains unchanged—or worse. However, there is no more antientrepreneurial attitude than acquiescence. The true entrepreneur never lets that happen. Rather than thinking about what the others should do, he thinks about what he can do, and he does it. And if it is possible to do this in business and in the search for professional success, why should it be different in social issues? That is the type of entrepreneurial vision Inemp intends to promote and stimulate.

Erring to Get It Right

* ✳ *

In conclusion, I would like to talk a little about erring and getting it right. Just like any human being, I have made many mistakes in my life. However, contrary to many, I do not worry about hiding them. In my previous books, *POI: The Power of Ideas* and *Stone Soup: Ten Ingredients for You to Create Your Recipe for Success*, I give details about some of them: initiatives that did not go forward, wrong evaluations of people and situations, ideas that did not get off the ground. And the reason I do not hide them is because I am not ashamed of them. I would have been ashamed if I had not tried out of fear of failure. The lessons I learned from my errors were and still are priceless. It is the experience you acquire trying and erring that paves the way for long-lasting success. He who achieves success without ever having made a mistake—if that is at all possible—does not have sufficient experience to deal with the mishaps and setbacks that sooner or later will come. People who never have the chance to learn from their small mistakes in life, end up erring when they cannot and with whom they should not. The medical student can make several mistakes during anatomy class. But the surgeon cannot make a mistake during surgery.

Malcolm Forbes, owner of the famous magazine that bears his last name, once wrote in his column in *Forbes* that "a vital ingredient for sustained success is occasional failure." He says, "There is nothing as essential as an unequivocal error of a certain magnitude to restore the necessary perspective to ensure long-lasting success." Forbes concludes his article saying that a big shot who has never made a major blunder—in his opinion, an isolated occurrence—is in the same disadvantageous position as the hen that never laid an egg and is now heading for the pot."[14] Therefore, if I were to add anything else to everything I have already said in this book about selling an idea in three minutes, I would say: learn from your errors and build your own baggage of knowledge, your own internal database that will feed your unconscious as well as your conscious mind and that will come to your aid whenever you need it.

It is very common to read reports in the newspapers such as: "surveys indicate that more than half of new businesses close within two years," and things of that nature. And then there are long lists of causes that range from the economic crisis to the businessperson's lack of planning. However, what these surveys normally do not reveal is what these businesspeople learned from their mistakes. Or how many times successful businesspeople failed and went through bankruptcies before getting it right. Many people are shocked when they read information about the percentage of people whose businesses did not work out. But wouldn't it be much worse if that percentage referred to those who hit rock bottom without ever trying something?

One of my objectives when I created Inemp was to develop and support surveys that show the other side, that value the experience of those who dared to try. After all, as Carl Gustav Jung once said, "Truth comes from error. That is why I was never afraid to err, nor did I ever seriously regret it."

---

[14] Peter Krass, *The Book of Business Wisdom*. New York: John Wiley, 1997.

BIBLIOGRAPHY

Bellino, Ricardo. *Midas & Sadim—Tudo o que Você Precisa Evitar Para Ter Sucesso e Nãose Tornar Um Sadim* (Midas & Sadim—Everything You Need to Know to Succeed and Not to Become a Sadim). Rio de Janeiro: Campus/Elsevier, 2005.

_____. *PDI—O Poder das Idéias. Como Transformar Idéias em Tacadas de Sucesso* (PDI—The Power of Ideas: How to Transform Ideas into Strokes of Success). Rio de Janeiro: Campus/Elsevier, 2003.

_____. *Sopa de Pedra—Dez Ingredientes Para Você Criar Sua Receita de Sucesso* (Stone Soup—Ten Ingredients for You to Create Your Recipe for Success). Rio de Janeiro: Campus/Elsevier, 2004.

Britto, Francisco and Wever, Luiz. *Empreendedores Brasileiros*, vols. 1 and 2. Rio de Janeiro: Campus/Elsevier, 2003/2004.

Floyd, Robbie Davies and Arvidson P. Sven. *Intuition: The Inside Story*. New York: Routledge, 1997.

Girard, Joe, and Brown, Stanley H. *How to Sell Anything to Anybody*. New York: Simon & Schuster, 1979.

Gladwell, Malcolm. *Blink: The Power of Thinking without Thinking.* New York: Little, Brown and Company, 2000.

_____. *The Tipping Point: How Little Things Can Make a Big Difference.* New York: Little, Brown and Company, 2005.

Krass, Peter. *The Book of Business Wisdom.* New York: John Wiley & Sons, 1997.

Piatelli-Palmarini, Massimo. *Inevitable Illusions: How Mistakes of Reason Rule Our Minds.* New York: John Wiley & Sons, 1994.

Wilson, Timothy D. *Strangers to Ourselves: Discovering the Adaptive Unconscious.* Cambridge, MA: Belknap Press of Harvard University Press, 2002.

INDEX

ABOUT THE AUTHOR

Ricardo Bellino is an international entrepreneur who brought Elite Models and The Look of the Year, the most famous modeling contest in the world, to Brazil. Now Bellino is the founder and dealmaker behind Trump Realty Brazil, an enterprise born from the creation of the largest golf complex in Latin America, Villa Trump. The author of three business books focusing on the power of ideas and sales techniques, Bellino is the first commercial partner of the Trump Organization outside the United States.